THE 2ND SS PANZER DIVISION DAS REICH

 CASEMATE | ILLUSTRATED

CASEMATE | ILLUSTRATED

THE 2ND SS PANZER DIVISION DAS REICH

YVES BUFFETAUT

CASEMATE | ILLUSTRATED
MILITARIA

Print Edition: ISBN 978-1-61200-5256
Digital Edition: ISBN 978-1-61200-5263

This book is published in cooperation with and under license from
Sophia Histoire & Collections. Originally published in French as
Militaria Hors-Serie No 97, © Histoire & Collections 2015

Typeset, design and additional material © Casemate Publishers 2018
Translation by Hannah McAdams
Design by Paul Hewitt, Battlefield Design
Color artwork by Eric Schwartz © Histoire & Collections
Photo retouching and separations by Remy Spezzano
Additional text by Steven Smith
Printed and bound by Megaprint, Turkey

CASEMATE PUBLISHERS (US)
Telephone (610) 853-9131
Fax (610) 853-9146
Email: casemate@casematepublishers.com
www.casematepublishers.com

CASEMATE PUBLISHERS (UK)
Telephone (01865) 241249
Fax (01865) 794449
Email: casemate-uk@casematepublishers.co.uk
www.casematepublishers.co.uk

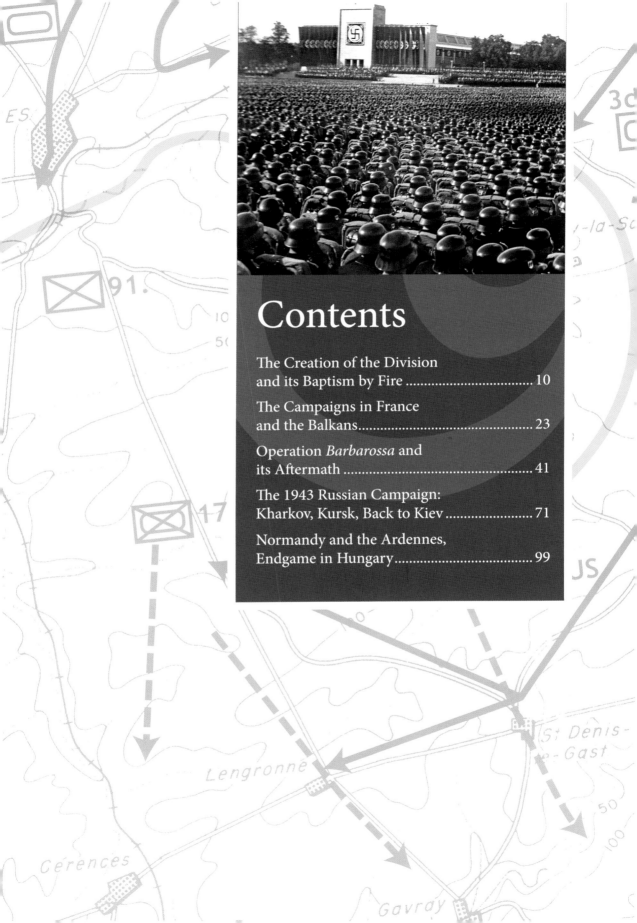

Contents

The Creation of the Division
and its Baptism by Fire 10

The Campaigns in France
and the Balkans.. 23

Operation *Barbarossa* and
its Aftermath 41

The 1943 Russian Campaign:
Kharkov, Kursk, Back to Kiev 71

Normandy and the Ardennes,
Endgame in Hungary... 99

Timeline of Events

SS-Das Reich fought throughout the war, from the invasion of Poland in 1939 to the last muscle-spasms of German defense in May 1945. More than any other division, save perhaps SS-Leibstandarte, it participated in every crisis of the war, and it had to be rebuilt time and again due to losses. Its ferocious combat power, whether applied in the East or the West, never came into question.

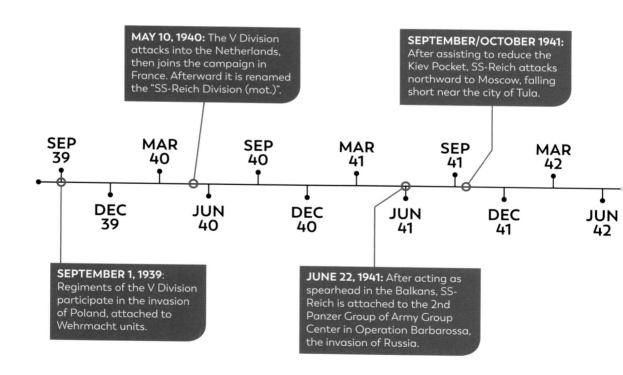

MAY 10, 1940: The V Division attacks into the Netherlands, then joins the campaign in France. Afterward it is renamed the "SS-Reich Division (mot.)".

SEPTEMBER/OCTOBER 1941: After assisting to reduce the Kiev Pocket, SS-Reich attacks northward to Moscow, falling short near the city of Tula.

SEP 39

MAR 40

SEP 40

MAR 41

SEP 41

MAR 42

DEC 39

JUN 40

DEC 40

JUN 41

DEC 41

JUN 42

SEPTEMBER 1, 1939: Regiments of the V Division participate in the invasion of Poland, attached to Wehrmacht units.

JUNE 22, 1941: After acting as spearhead in the Balkans, SS-Reich is attached to the 2nd Panzer Group of Army Group Center in Operation Barbarossa, the invasion of Russia.

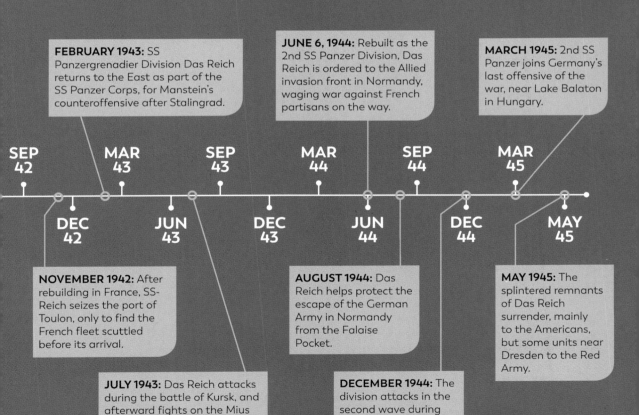

FEBRUARY 1943: SS Panzergrenadier Division Das Reich returns to the East as part of the SS Panzer Corps, for Manstein's counteroffensive after Stalingrad.

JUNE 6, 1944: Rebuilt as the 2nd SS Panzer Division, Das Reich is ordered to the Allied invasion front in Normandy, waging war against French partisans on the way.

MARCH 1945: 2nd SS Panzer joins Germany's last offensive of the war, near Lake Balaton in Hungary.

SEP 42 — MAR 43 — SEP 43 — MAR 44 — SEP 44 — MAR 45

DEC 42 — JUN 43 — DEC 43 — JUN 44 — DEC 44 — MAY 45

NOVEMBER 1942: After rebuilding in France, SS-Reich seizes the port of Toulon, only to find the French fleet scuttled before its arrival.

AUGUST 1944: Das Reich helps protect the escape of the German Army in Normandy from the Falaise Pocket.

MAY 1945: The splintered remnants of Das Reich surrender, mainly to the Americans, but some units near Dresden to the Red Army.

JULY 1943: Das Reich attacks during the battle of Kursk, and afterward fights on the Mius and through the following winter during Army Group South's strategic withdrawal.

DECEMBER 1944: The division attacks in the second wave during the Battle of the Bulge, in inconclusive combat.

7

During the earlier days of the Nazi Party rallies at Nuremberg, the call of the standards of the different movements—SA, SS, NSKK, NSSK, and others—was always a sight to behold, if only for its spectacular staging. Here the SS demonstrate their mastery of weapons handling and drill in a carefully planned parade. (BA, Bild 183-H12148, Scherl)

Men of the Verfügungstruppe during maneuvers before the war. They are wearing steel helmets from World War I. (Lemo)

The Creation of the Division and its Baptism by Fire

In the early days, the Schützstaffel, or SS, was simply a security service that protected the officials of the Nazi Party—NSDAP—against attacks by their opponents, notably the communists of the KPD. From little more than a group of Bavarian bouncers in the 1920s, the Munich-based SS would, over the following years, become a veritable army within an army, their role continuing to grow until Nazi Germany's final collapse in 1945. Arguably the most emblematic unit of the SS was the Das Reich Division.

Providing protection for Hitler and the other officials of the Nazi Party initially only required a handful of men, but as the NSDAP became increasingly established in German political life and expanded well beyond the borders of Bavaria, more and more men were needed. They were given paramilitary training and uniforms; soon they were paid directly by the party, after it had representatives, or "deputies," in the Reichstag. It was no longer a mere security service, but a veritable private militia, housed in barrack-like lodgings.

For a while, the SS groups were renamed "Politische Bereitschaften" (roughly, "political readiness units"), which demonstrates the political character of their paramilitary role. It is notable that in the early years, the other branch of the SS, the Allgemeine SS—or General SS—did not have that same paramilitary element. It was the Politische Bereitschaften that would ultimately be transformed into the Waffen-SS, though lines between the two branches during World War II would sometimes become blurred.

Reichsführer SS Heinrich Himmler. The title, meaning "Head of the SS" was purely political and did not imply any operational command role. It was created in 1926 and only five men held it, of whom Himmler (1929–45) was the most famous. (Rights reserved)

In Profile:
Heinrich Himmler

A true mystery in history, Himmler became the second most powerful man in the Third Reich, despite a personage that by no means resembled the Aryan ideal he was so fanatic to pursue. General Guderian, for one, could not figure him out, calling him "the most impenetrable of all Hitler's disciples," though he said he also "went out of his way to be polite."

As head of the SS, Himmler constructed a vast empire of murder, persecution, surveillance, and foreign intelligence, beginning with the decapitation of his rival organization, the SA, in the "Night of the Long Knives" in 1934. The only one of his creations that wasn't cloaked in secrecy was the Waffen-SS, which earned renown for battlefield courage throughout the war.

In 1961 Albert Speer—Hitler's architect and economic czar—became the West's favorite Nazi with his memoir, "Inside the Third Reich." Less well known is Speer's final book, "Infiltration," subtitled "How Heinrich Himmler Schemed to Build an SS Industrial Empire," in which we learn of even greater ambitions on the part of the Reichsführer SS. Himmler committed suicide after the Third Reich's fall, so we can still only speculate how a man so apparently nondescript became such a power, and a menace.

Hitler Comes to Power

On January 30th, 1933, the previous chaotic state of German politics came to a head. In 1932, the desperate economic situation in Germany—due in part to heavy reparations the country was forced to pay by the Treaty of Versailles in the aftermath of World War I—combined with a nationwide sense of frustration and discontent, provided the perfect catalyst for Adolf Hitler's rise to power. His movement swept across Germany, using his charismatic personality and oratory skills to gain political support. In the election held in July of that year, the NSDAP won 230 seats in the Reichstag.

The breaking point for the German parliament came early the following year. In January 1933, the German President Paul von Hindenburg, intimidated by Hitler's growing popularity and the thuggish nature of his cadre of supporters, the SA (or Brownshirts), initially refused to make him Chancellor, despite it being the obvious move and the will of the people. Even though the NSDAP had lost some ground compared to previous elections, it nevertheless remained the primary party in Germany in terms of number of deputies. The President eventually gave in after a series of complex negotiations involving ex-Chancellor Franz von Papen, a group of wealthy businessmen and the right-wing German National People's Party (DNVP), and on January 30th, 1933, Hitler was named Chancellor. His rise to power was not, as many believe, a military coup, but actually a combination of democratic process and public pressure—a disturbing thought.

An SS detachment passes through the Brandenburg Gate, saluted by a crowd of Berliners shortly after Hitler's ascension to the position of Chancellor in 1933. (Lemo)

Even before the Nazi Party came to power, the SS had become a separate body within the organization of the NSDAP, functioning (albeit unofficially) as a kind of police force for the party and its associates.

A guard of the SS Deutschland Regiment in front of Munich's Ehrentempel—a mausoleum erected in 1935 in memory of 16 Nazi Party activists who were killed during an attempted coup on November 8th/9th, 1923.

What followed, however, was less democratic, though it exceeds the scope of this study. Insofar as the SS is concerned, however, Hitler continued to establish his authority: the Allgemeine SS began to permeate all aspects of daily life in Germany, while the ranks of political paramilitary detachments, the Politische Bereitschaften, continued to grow and infiltrate the larger German towns in order to prevent any counter-revolutionary attempts (the NSDAP was at this time seen as a revolutionary party). This rapid development necessitated a reorganization of the SS.

On December 14th, 1934, under the supervision of Reichsführer SS Heinrich Himmler, the former Politische Bereitschaften—including Hitler's personal bodyguard, the Leibstandarte Adolf Hitler—was reorganized into units of a purely military nature, the Verfügungstruppe (Combat Support Force, or literally "dispositional troops," i.e. at Hitler's personal disposal).

The structure of the Verfügungstruppe (VT) was replicated from that of the army, with each regiment made up of a number of battalions. Special names were given to its organizations in order to differentiate them from the army proper. The sub-units were not,

A shot taken during the Reichsparteitag (Rally of Victory) in 1938. Physical fitness was highly valued by the Nazi regime, and the first members of the SS were genuine athletes.

therefore, regiments per se, but *standarten*, even though, subsequently and for simplification, the term "regiment" reappeared later.

There were three original standarten:

- SS Leibstandarte Adolf Hitler—LSSAH or LAH, for short—which was based at Berlin-Lichterfelde and recruited its men from military regions I, II, III, IV and VIII, as well as any German national over the height of 1.78 meters;

- I. SS Standarte Deutschland/VT, in Munich, recruiting from military regions V, VII and XII;

- II. SS Standarte Germania/VT, in Hamburg-Veddel, recruiting from military regions VI, IX, X and XI.

After the Anschluss—Germany's annexation of Austria in March 1938—a new standarte was created:

- III. SS Standarte Der Führer, based in Vienna and recruited in Austria, which the Nazis called Ostmark in order to distance itself from the old Austrian Empire.

These units were viewed with wariness by the German regular army, or *Heer*; it would take time, and proven performance on the battlefield, before they became integral parts of military operations.

Map of military regions

The Nazis knew how to put on a show, especially for the parades and rallies at Nuremberg, where the black uniforms of the SS seemed particularly impressive. The director of *Star Wars*, George Lucas, was reportedly inspired by the SS when creating his own "stormtroopers." (Rights reserved)

The Initial SS Division

In 1935, Hitler unilaterally terminated the Treaty of Versailles, to re-establish an unfettered military program in Germany. He planned a peacetime army of 36 divisions, of which one would be an SS formation. Named the V Division (Verfügungs), its strength was not to exceed 20,000 men. The introduction of this SS division was not exactly welcomed by the army, which could hardly have wished for such political intrusion. At first the army denied it certain specialized training and support services that would allow the V Division to operate independently. In a further attempt to distinguish the SS from the *Heer*, the ranks of the SS were displayed on the men's sleeves, while those of the army were worn on their epaulettes.

The initial SS division was composed of the three regiments cited above, Deutschland, Germania, and Der Führer; the Leibstandarte SS Adolf Hitler was excluded from forming its own division until later. It was primarily the Deutschland regiment that would form the basis of the 2nd SS Division Das Reich.

Formation of the Deutschland Regiment

In October 1933, the first battalion of what would become the Deutschland Regiment was established, though it was modest in both size and scope. Thirty-five men were chosen from among the standarte of the Allgemeine SS to become the unit's officers; they attended the first SS officer "school" at Bald Tölz, in Bavaria, which had only recently opened. These men were then followed by the troops, who also came from the Allgemeine SS. It was decided at the outset that these men would form SS squads within police companies.

The term Waffen-SS, which was extended to all military formations of the SS, ostensibly appeared for the first time in one of Himmler's memoranda, dated November 2nd, 1939, after the outbreak of war between Germany and Poland.

As the number of these squads grew rapidly, a detachment known as the Politische Bereitshaft München (Munich) was formed. It was a battalion in the true sense of the word, with three companies of infantry, one of machine-gunners and one of artillery. Its head, Ritter von Hengl, came from the police, and brought with him police officers to supervise the new unit, essentially composed of southern Germans.

In October 1934, this first battalion joined two others to form a standarte, and took the name 1st Regiment SS-VT. During the course of the Nuremberg rallies over the next few years, the new standarte developed into the Deutschland Regiment and received armbands bearing its new name.

The 1st Battalion established itself at the Freimann barracks in Munich in 1936, where it was joined by the regimental staff at the beginning of summer 1939. Training in the battalion was mostly based on parade drill and physical conditioning, as the unit was principally used for ceremonial duties and shows of force. Military training in terms of actual combat was a secondary consideration.

Midday at Berlin-Lichterfelde when the guard is relieved and their uniforms inspected, at the Leibstandarte Adolf Hitler barracks, November 22nd, 1938. (BA, Bild 183-H15390, o. Ang.)

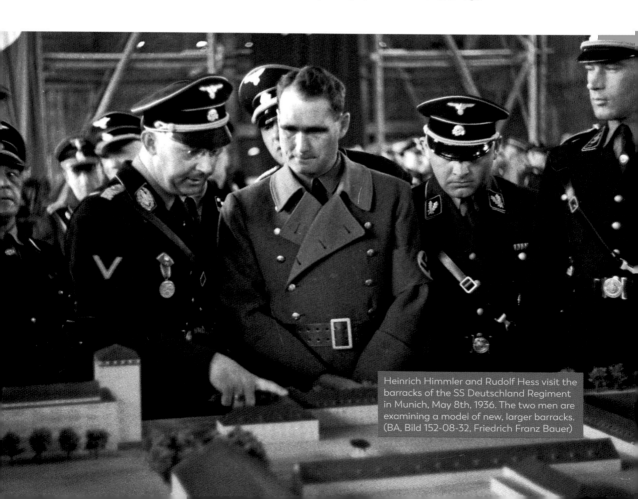

Heinrich Himmler and Rudolf Hess visit the barracks of the SS Deutschland Regiment in Munich, May 8th, 1936. The two men are examining a model of new, larger barracks. (BA, Bild 152-08-32, Friedrich Franz Bauer)

A senior officer of the SS Deutschland Regiment greets the Führer during a military ceremony, well before the beginning of the war.

The 2nd Battalion, formed in 1933, was much worse off, as it had practically no money; its financial situation was so poor that the men did not even have uniforms until March 1934. The recruits came principally from Austria, where the machinations of the Nazi Party were initially unpopular, forcing some militants into exile. This strong Austrian connection led the authorities to name the battalion the Austrian Legion, before giving it several other names related to Austria. This only lasted for a short time, as Mussolini, a vocal supporter of Austrian independence, demanded that all Austrian units and militias in Germany be dissolved. To avoid this, Himmler gave German citizenship to all Austrians serving in the 2nd Battalion. On April 1st, 1935, the Austrian Legion became the 2nd Battalion of the Deutschland Regiment, based at Ingolstadt under the command of Karl-Maria Demelhüber.

Strangely, the 3rd Battalion appeared *after* the 4th did. It was formed on July 1st, 1936, using the framework of the 1st and 4th Battalions, with volunteers from Bavaria and Munich.

Volunteers from Würtemberg made up the 4th Battalion, whose structure was based closely on that of an army battalion. Laced with Great War veterans, it was, without doubt, the battalion that received the best military training, and, on November 1st, 1938, it left the Deutschland Regiment to become a separate motorcycle battalion.

War

During the summer of 1939, the troops of the V units were optimistic. The young SS troopers were convinced that Hitler would achieve in Poland what he had accomplished with the Sudetenland at the Munich conference: the Western allies would bow to Germany's superior might once again. After all, what Frenchman or Englishman would really want to die for Danzig?

Contrary to popular belief, Polish cavalry never charged the panzers. However, it often intervened against the German artillery, as the SS Deutschland Regiment found out to its cost. (Rights reserved)

In September 1939, the German Army was not exactly "motorized," and the panzer divisions had far too many light tanks to be truly effective. The SS Deutschland Regiment was no exception. This may explain the excellent resistance of the Polish army, despite being effectively abandoned by the Western Allies. (Rights reserved)

Stormtroopers are presented with awards at the end of the campaign in France. Armbands are worn by men of the Leibstandarte Adolf Hitler. (BA, Bild 101III-Lerche-46-02-2, Lerche)

By mid-August, the Deutschland Regiment found itself in East Prussia for the commemorations of the 25th anniversary of the Battle of Tannenberg. It received the order to put itself at the disposal of the East Prussia Panzer Unit, or Panzer Division "Kempf," which itself fell under Army Group North (von Bock); elsewhere, the Germania Regiment was placed under command of VIII Army Corps, south of the frontier.

Hostilities looked set to begin on August 26th, 1939, but at the last moment Hitler suspended the invasion of Poland after learning of the Anglo-Polish Agreement—providing for mutual assistance in case of invasion by Germany—which might have led to a diplomatic opening. However, it was not easy to halt the march of several armies; the Polish realized that an attack was imminent and therefore mobilized on August 30th. Hitler renewed his order to invade the next day, discarding any further thoughts of diplomacy.

On September 1st, Panzer Division Kempf attacked Poland from East Prussia, breaking through the defensive line of Mlava (named after a frontier village), with the Deutschland Regiment in the van preparing the ground for the panzers.

The assault planned against the small town of Zacrozym and the Modlin Fortress near Warsaw on September 29th at 0530hrs was suspended at the last minute for an hour due to a rumor that the defenders had surrendered, but of course they had not. At 0615hrs, the artillery began its shelling, and at 0630hrs, the companies crossed their start line, preceded by flamethrower detachments. Zacrozym was taken in half an hour. The defense became disorderly, as an order to surrender had been transmitted to some troops but not others. The fighting was confused, but it quickly became clear that the troops occupying Modlin Fortress were continuing the fight. German artillery recommenced its bombardment, complemented by Ju-87 "Stuka" dive-bombers. At 1400hrs, the defenders yielded.

The fall of Modlin marked the end of the Deutschland Regiment's brief role in the Polish campaign. On October 19th, the different regiments were brought together in the V Division, which was good news for the troops, as fighting within a large unit with a common origin was preferable to serving as an appendage to an alien division. In reality, things were much more complicated…

The Campaigns in France and the Balkans

In November 1939, the SS Verfügungs Division found itself in Czechoslovakia, before being transferred to the west of Germany for six months. There, it went through intensive training to prepare for the offensive against France—something that had been playing on everyone's mind since the Führer had failed to re-establish diplomatic relations with France and Britain. The winter and spring were employed to reinforce the division and perfect the training of the large number of new recruits.

A Horch 108 towing a 37mm Pak gun during the Balkans campaign of 1941. The men aboard appear to be from the SS-Leibstandarte. (Rights reserved)

In Profile:
The V Division in France 1940

SS 2057

A Mittlerer Einheits-PKW Horch 901 Kfz 15. The V Division was an infantry division, without armored vehicles and thus essentially horse-powered. The Horch 901 was a general staff vehicle built by Auto-Union that served on all fronts.

Eingew
Nutzlas
oder
Last gle

A Phänomen Granit 25H-Sanitäts medical vehicle. Originally a civilian truck dating from 1931, it was converted in 1936 into an ambulance for the Wehrmacht.

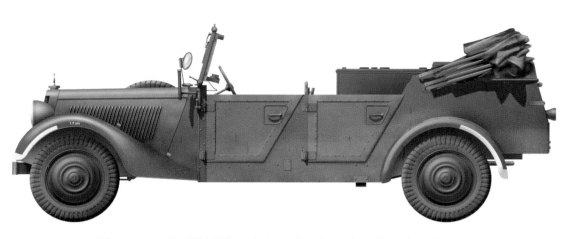

A V Division Mercedes 170 VK. This vehicle was based directly on the civilian 170 V car, which means it was not particularly well adapted to all-terrain driving.

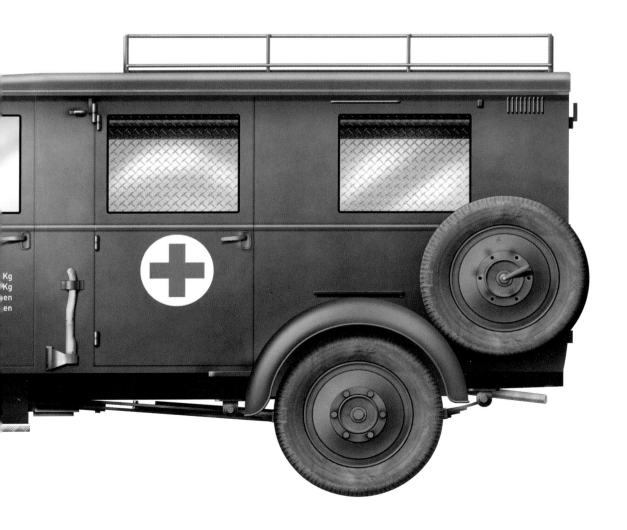

A group of stormtroopers in May 1940. If we zoomed in on this image, we would be able to read on the men's armbands that they are part of the Deutschland Regiment. They are posing in front of a Mercedes L 3000 truck. (Rights reserved)

BA, Bild 183-R97166/o.Ang.

In Profile:
General Paul Hausser

More than any man, Paul Hausser shaped the nascent Waffen-SS into a fighting force that would not only earn the respect of the German Army but its opponents in the battles that followed.

A decorated commander in the Great War, Hausser stayed in the Reichswehr until 1932, resigning as a general. Afterward he joined the Nazi Party, given its promise to resurrect Germany, and became the senior officer in the Waffen-SS.

He led the Reich (V) Division through France, the Balkans, and the initial stages of Barbarossa, and then commanded the SS Panzer Corps in the 1943 battles of Kharkov and Kursk. In Normandy he took command of the Seventh Army during its moment of greatest crisis, and toward the end of the war commanded Army Group G.

If "Papa" Hausser had not been badly wounded in Russia (losing an eye), and then in Normandy (carried out of Falaise on the back of a tank), Hausser would doubtless have led Sixth SS Panzer Army in the Ardennes offensive. Had that been the case the Germans' northern wing in the Battle of the Bulge would surely have performed better than it did under Sepp Dietrich (an excellent division commander but over his head in army command).

Hausser survived the war, and after withstanding recriminations at Nuremburg, went on to become a lead spokesman for the honor of the Waffen-SS. Right up until his death in 1972 he fervently maintained that his men were battlefield soldiers only, unconnected to the darker side of Hitler's regime.

If the officers and men of V Division had hoped to serve within their own SS division, they would have been sorely disappointed, as during the next campaign the regiments and battalions were separated once more and attached to other divisions to improve efficiency.

The V Division was made a component of the Eighteenth Army, which was first directed against the Netherlands. Only two sub-units were engaged during the first wave of attack on May 10th, 1940: the Deutschland Regiment and the Aufklärungsabteilung (reconnaissance battalion). Kampfgruppe Grave consisted of this battalion, a battalion of Wehrmacht machine-gunners and a battalion of artillery. This battle group was then divided into five assault detachments charged with seizing the bridge over the Waal at Nijmegen, and bridges over canals in four other locations. Only the bridge at Heuman was captured intact, but at Hatert, the Dutch blew up the bridge without destroying it completely. The first SS assault was swept away by enemy fire and the entire detachment was either killed or wounded, with the exception of Untersturmführer Demelhüber and four men who finally managed to seize the bridge. On May 11th, the reconnaissance battalion returned to the V Division.

The SS at the Ijssel

The Der Führer Regiment in its baptism of fire also attacked at zero hour with the 207th Infantry Division. Within two hours, its 3rd Battalion had arrived at the banks of the Ijssel, near Arnhem. All the bridges over the river had been blown, but at 1300hrs, the 2nd Battalion succeeded in crossing the river and establishing a bridgehead. The strongpoints at Werstervoort were captured and the town of Arnhem soon fell. The Ijssel defensive line, which the Dutch had wanted to hold for three days, fell in just four hours.

On May 13th, the Der Führer Regiment participated in the breakthrough of the second Dutch defensive line, Grebe, and then headed off in the direction of Utrecht before reaching the North Sea between Ijmuiden and Zandvoort.

During this time, the bulk of the SS V Division was held in reserve, without taking part in the fighting. It was then directed to the coast of Holland, to seize the island of Walcheren where the French Seventh Army had deployed. Though the Dutch army surrendered quickly, on May 14th, the same could not be said of French troops still in Dutch territory.

The SS at Walcheren

It was the (as yet untested in battle) Deutschland Regiment that was engaged on May 16th to capture Walcheren, a veritable island, connected to the mainland only by dikes and causeways, at the strategic mouth of the Scheldt. The regiment was formed into two battle groups with one led by Kleinheisterkamp's 3rd Battalion and the other by Witt's 1st Battalion. The 3rd led the attack, followed by the 1st, moving from one landfall to the next by advancing along a road built on a dike. This modus operandi was not a good one for the assailants, as they were faced with determined adversaries who could concentrate their fire on the single road. Indeed, the French (and the Dutch, before their surrender) had had time to install barbed wire and minefields along the dike before the Germans arrived. Seventeen Waffen-SS stormtroopers were killed during the approach.

In Profile:
SS Reich Division, Invasion of the French Free Zone, *la Zone Libre* (or "Vichy")

A Panzer III Ausf L armed with a 50mm long cannon, capable of destroying any Allied tank of the time, November 1942.

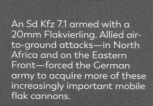

An Sd Kfz 7.1 armed with a 20mm Flakvierling. Allied air-to-ground attacks—in North Africa and on the Eastern Front—forced the German army to acquire more of these increasingly important mobile flak cannons.

A Panzer IV Ausf F2 of the SS Reich Division during the capture of the Toulon naval base, at the time when the division was being transformed into a panzergrenadier division. It was called to the Russian front soon afterwards.

A rare photograph of the Waffen-SS in a Dutch town in May 1940. These are men of the Der Führer Regiment, V Division. The armband on the tunic of the officer pointing at something out-of-shot can be seen quite clearly; another of the men is dressed in a camouflage uniform.

Paul Schümann, 9th Company, 3rd Battalion, wrote:

> We waited for the order to attack. "Now—get up!" And we charged right into the line of fire. As soon as our comrades reached the road on the dike, they were struck down by machine guns, antitank cannons and artillery fire. Each step brought us closer to the enemy. We just had to get near enough to use our hand grenades.
>
> While we were attacking, I saw a man fall, then two others to my right, then the soldier beside me was suddenly face-down on the ground. Some of the men were tearing open the dressings with their teeth in a desperate attempt to patch up their shattered arms and cover the gaping holes their chests.
>
> It was a massacre. Our gunners were killed one after the other, at such a rate that we had to continually replace them.
>
> A cry rang out: "Bring a machine gun to the front!" Horn, my number two, stood up then immediately fell down again, screaming in pain. I tried to help

The German Army, including the V Division, was still largely a horse-drawn operation in May 1940. In this photo taken through a window by a Dutch civilian, we can see a traffic jam of horse-drawn carriages in the suburbs of La Haye. (Rights reserved)

The 1940 itinerary of the SS V Division through the Netherlands reads like the reverse of the Allies' Operation *Market Garden* four years later, including the same task of seizing bridges and with familiar place names like Arnhem, Nijmegen, and Eindhoven. In both campaigns Walcheren proved a key location and a tough nut to crack, especially so for the Allies as it controlled access to the port of Antwerp. Antwerp was desperately needed by the Allies in 1944 to solve their supply problems, but it cost them over 12,000 men to recapture it.

A Dutch airfield defender in May 1940. The German advance into the Netherlands was so fast that the Dutch army was forced to surrender within just four days. Yet even within that short period, Dutch antiaircraft fire took a significant toll of German transport planes. (Rights reserved)

him, but it was too late. He had been hit right in the stomach. On my right, a man lay on his back, his fingers clawing at the air. It was Unterscharführer Vonscheidt. The sun caught on a ribbon on his tunic—the Iron Cross he'd won in Poland.

Our 9th Company was recalled from combat. We retreated slowly … half an hour later, the enemy had withdrawn behind the dike. The fight had killed 17 of our men and wounded 30 more. That bloody May 17th ended when night fell.

French Armor Fights Back

The Deutschland Regiment failed to seize Walcheren, but the island nevertheless fell to the Wehrmacht not long afterwards.

The SS V Division then received the order to deploy to France, to support the 6th and 8th panzer divisions pushing for Calais. The SS were then ordered to secure the canal at La Bassée to prevent retreating Allied troops from reaching Dunkirk.

Once again, the division did not fight as a unit; its regiments were divided up and allotted to other divisions. The Der Führer Regiment took up positions in the Aire-sur-la-Lys sector, where, on May 23rd, just before sunrise, it was attacked by French tanks. The 10th and 11th companies were surrounded, while the 5th and 7th companies counterattacked at approximately 0400hrs. A chaotic night-time battle ensued, neither side knowing the exact position of the other, columns intersecting, splitting and meeting unexpectedly. This resulted in substantial losses on both sides.

Hauptscharführer Röske, who served in the radio detachment of the 2nd Battalion, Artillery Regiment, V Division, was surprised by the French attack:

> A little before daybreak, at around 4 o'clock, I was awoken by a sentinel yelling, "Stabscharführer, the French are here!" I jumped out of the truck, grabbing my gun. I heard the calls of other sentinels—"Achtung! Achtung!"—and the sound of shooting.
>
> At that moment, the light improved and we were able to understand what was happening. I jumped into the shelter and found myself beside an Obersturmführer who had just received a message from a motorcycle courier telling us we were surrounded. The Der Führer Regiment were preparing to break through when a shower of bullets came through and injured the officer in both thighs. I carried him to the help station, where ten of his comrades were already being treated.
>
> When I left the place, I heard someone asking for the radio detachment to send a message for help. That was my job, so I began to crawl towards a radio-equipped truck. As soon as I reached it, a Frenchman came towards me with his hands in the air. I signalled to him to get down, but it was too late, and he was shot. I opened the truck door, and a group of French soldiers suddenly attacked from a hedge, though they didn't reach me. Another burst of gunfire, coming from a different direction, mowed them down. I later learned that the shots had been fired by a group of men from Der Führer who had taken up position in a neighboring farm.

Finally, the Germans managed to repel the French, but not without difficulty, as the German 37mm antitank guns were no match for the Renault R35 tanks. In the end, the 3rd Battalion, Der Führer had to destroy the tanks with explosive charges, putting 13 out of action. One R35 was destroyed at point-blank range, just five meters from the antitank gun. Five hundred French soldiers were captured.

Looking for the British in the Nieppe Forest

On May 27th at 0830hrs, the Germania and Der Führer regiments, alongside the reconnaissance group, were engaged in the Nieppe Forest to drive the 2nd British Infantry Division away from the area. The battle lasted an entire day and Germania experienced huge difficulties advancing in the face of fire from the Queen's Own Royal West Kent Regiment. The army corps demanded a more efficient advance the next day. It was much easier going for the Germans the following morning, as the Belgian Army surrendered on May 28th, opening up the northern flank of the British Expeditionary Force, which then quickly fell back to Dunkirk.

A period of relative calm followed for the V Division, which contented itself with following the British and French retreats. On June 1st, it received reinforcements of 2,000 officers and men to replace those lost in May.

During the Battle of France, the V Division did not participate in the breakthrough of the Weygand line, but did shadow the retreating French forces. The division passed through Orléans, Tours, Poitiers, and Angoulême, with only brief skirmishes with the French to punctuate an otherwise uneventful advance.

After the armistice, the V Division returned to the Netherlands to assist in the demobilization and disarmament of the Dutch army. There, the division underwent a number of structural changes, with the Germania Regiment and some other units being hived off to form a new division, the SS Wiking. The commander of the Deutschland Regiment, Brigadeführer Steiner, became the first head of Wiking.

Next, the V Division left for Vesoul in eastern France. On December 3rd, 1940, it received an order from Reichsführer Heinrich Himmler to rename itself SS Division Deutschland, but Himmler quickly changed his mind and, in January, it was instead renamed SS Division Reich (mot.). The regiments were restructured and the division received a self-propelled artillery battery as well as a motorcycle battalion. By March 1941, the division was considered capable of serving as a fully motorized unit.

A reconnaissance battalion motorized column in Yugoslavia. We can see from the bumper marking of the six-wheeled Sd Kfz that it does not belong to the Waffen-SS. (Rights reserved)

On to Yugoslavia

On April 6th, the division began a transfer from France, to western Romania, as the theater of war was now expanding to Yugoslavia and Greece.

On the 9th, the division received an order to send out its reconnaissance battalion to find passage over the Danube, in order to reach Belgrade more quickly, as the OKW (the German high command) believed that capturing the Yugoslav capital would trigger an immediate collapse of its army. Priority would be given to the German unit that reached the Alibunar–Belgrade road the fastest, which in turn meant that this unit would have the honor of taking the city. In response, Paul Hausser, commander of the Reich Division, challenged his troops to show him what they were capable of. It wasn't an easy feat, as before reaching the highway, the division had to advance over difficult terrain, peppered with marshes and bad roads.

On April 11th at 0905hrs, the advance began. Many of the vehicles got bogged down, but others pressed onwards, led by the motorcyclists who progressed quickly by making use of railway lines and drainage dikes. At 1730hrs, the Deutschland Regiment managed to regroup all its battalions at Alibunar, ahead of the other units of the army corps: the road to Belgrade was now open to them.

The troops, however, were exhausted, and couldn't leave as quickly as they had planned. The army corps authorized the division to halt its march upon reaching the Danube, without trying to establish a bridgehead on the opposite bank.

Apparently, this order did not reach Hauptsturmführer Fritz Klingenberg, who commanded the 2nd Company of the motorcycle battalion. He found a motorized dinghy and brought ten men (and their motorcycles) over to the south bank of the Danube. The company moved quickly towards the city. When they reached it, Klingenberg set up two machine-gun nests near the German embassy, poised for action.

Bluff at Belgrade

With the help of the German military attaché in Belgrade, Captain Klingenberg orchestrated a careful bluff. The attaché summoned the mayor of the city, one Jevrem Tomić, to the German embassy, and introduced him to the SS officer as being the head of a large German formation about to enter the capital. Klingenberg then presented the mayor with an ultimatum, according to which Belgrade would be subjected to a massive Luftwaffe bombardment if it did not surrender immediately. At 1845hrs, April 12th, 1941, the mayor relented and formally surrendered the city to a detachment of ten German motorcyclists. The Slavs would have been of a much different mindset the next morning when they discovered the deception, but during the night an armored detachment from the 11th Panzer Division entered the city, reinforcing the motorcyclists. That day, Tomić was replaced as mayor.

On April 18th, Yugoslavia surrendered totally, leaving many German units free to move on to Greece, after which no further enemies remained on the European mainland. As it was no longer considered possible to invade Britain, the Waffen-SS thought that they would be engaged with the British in the deserts of North Africa in support of Rommel's Afrikakorps. They never imagined that Hitler would be brave–or foolhardy enough–to invade the Soviet Union.

In Profile:
SS Reich Division, Operation Barbarossa

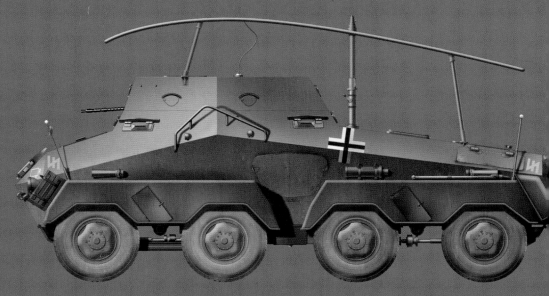

An eight-wheel Sd Kfz 263, equipped with a rooftop antenna.
This vehicle belonged to the reconnaissance battalion, and was
in particular demand during Operation *Barbarossa*.

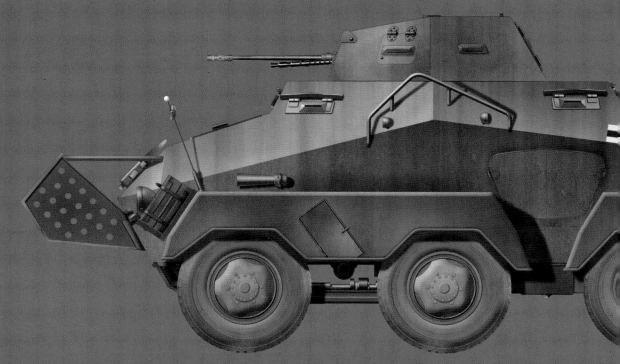

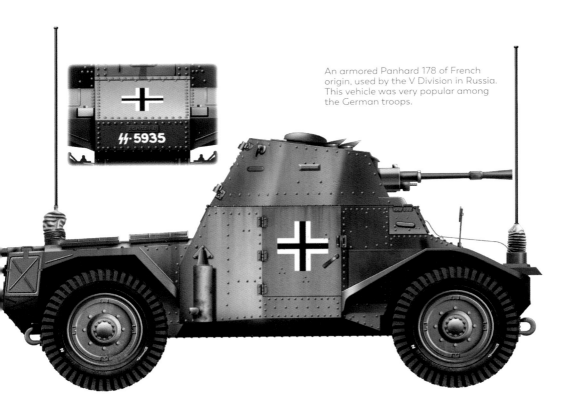

An armored Panhard 178 of French origin, used by the V Division in Russia. This vehicle was very popular among the German troops.

SS-5935

An armored Sd Kfz 231 of the reconnaissance battalion, V Division during the summer and autumn of 1941 in Russia.

Vehicles

As a motorized division, SS-Reich possessed a variety of specialized combat vehicles, aside from its motorcycles, kubelwagens, and troop-carrying lorries. The primitive Russian road network, however, proved a fierce foe of mobility, especially when rain turned the unpaved routes to mud, and then snow obscured them altogether. The Germans would increasingly rely on tracked vehicles for their operations in Russia.

Dessna Brücke
»Zum letzten Rennen«
erbaut
von
Pi.Btl.48

An SS Reich Division vehicle crosses the Desna on a bridge built by Pioneer Battalion 48. Note that the vehicle has a large G painted on it, which stands for Panzer Group Guderian. Also visible is the divisional insignia, and that of the reconnaissance battalion. (BA, Bild 101III-Zschaeckel-150-26)

Operation Barbarossa
and its Aftermath

Stormtroopers of the Waffen-SS prepare to fire a mortar. Though it is not immediately evident from this photograph, these men belong to the SS Wiking Division. (Rights reserved)

SS-Wiking

Before and at the start of World War II, the German Army was wary of competition with the Waffen-SS, and compelled Hitler to restrict its recruitment. Thus the first SS divisions were drawn from Hitler's own bodyguard (Leibstandarte), Nazi Party volunteers (Das Reich), the concentration camp system (Totenkopf), and the SS-controlled police (Polizei).

After the French campaign the SS discovered a new source of manpower in ethnic Germans abroad (not subject to Army recruitment) and foreigners who shared Nazi ideals. Thus the 5th SS Division, Wiking, was born constructed around Das Reich's Germania Regiment and filled out with Dutch, Flemish, Danish, and Scandinavian volunteers. Wiking's initial commander was Felix Steiner, former head of the V Division's Deutschland Regiment.

The superb performance of SS-Wiking in Russia opened the floodgates to further units of this type, drawing on foreign nationals, until in Paul Hausser's view, the Waffen-SS became Europe's "first international army."

When Operation Barbarossa—the Nazi invasion of the USSR—began on June 22nd, 1941, the Waffen-SS comprised three complete divisions, a little over 60,000 men. By 1945, when the Soviets overwhelmed the last German defenses in Berlin, the Waffen-SS had become a veritable army within an army, with 38 divisions and a million troops: it was on the Eastern Front that it saw this enormous growth. It was also here that the Reich Division was transformed into a powerful armored division, the 2nd SS Panzer Division, Das Reich.

In May 1941, the SS Reich Division found itself in Austria. No one really knew what the future held when superior officers were summoned to a conference at Gmunden am Traunsee in Upper Austria where they learned that Germany was going to attack Russia. One officer present at the meeting recalled the event: "There was no enthusiastic cry of 'Sieg Heil' when it was announced, because everyone felt so worried at the idea of invading a country of such size."

The men and the subordinate officers were not told what was happening; when the division left for Poland, the rumor was that they were crossing the USSR to attack British India from the north.

The SS Reich Division was put under command of the XXIV Army Corps, part of General Heinz Guderian's 2nd Panzer Group in Army Group Center, attacking across the front above the Pripet marshes in Belarus.

However, on June 22nd, 1941, the SS were not on the front line, nor were they even at the frontier. Rather, they were regulating road traffic between the Vistula and Bug rivers. At the time, the army still did not have confidence in the SS units, and was reluctant to give them a role in front-line action.

When, finally, the Reich Division was authorized to enter the Soviet Union, it found the roads reserved exclusively for the Wehrmacht, leaving the SS grenadiers to march on the verges.

The first objective was not given to the division until June 28th. The bulk of the division was ordered to cross a watercourse while a battle group—made up of the reconnaissance battalion, a motorcycle battalion and some Flak and engineering elements—took the main road to reach the region around Sloutsk, Belarus. Progress was fast, perhaps a little too fast, as the men of the motorcycle battalion soon found themselves surrounded and cut off from the rest of the division. The 3rd Battalion, Deutschland Regiment was called to their aid and intervened with self-propelled guns—75mm Ausf B StuG IIIs—named Yorck, Ziethen, Schill and Lützow. Their first engagement was, to the surprise of their critics, very favorable. Yorck put five Russian tanks out of action, and Schill four, not counting several antitank guns. The motorcycle battalion was relieved, but it had taken the 3rd Battalion to get them out of the mess they had got themselves into.

A Sturmgeschütz of the Reich Division on the outskirts of a Russian village in flames. For a long time, eight StuG III Ausf Bs were the only armored vehicles in the division that were capable of taking on Russian tanks. (BA, Bild 101I-596-0395-29, Ohlenbostel)

Heid Rühl, an artilleryman of the SS Reich Division, recalled how the subsequent advance unfolded. The troops reached the city of Minsk and then continued in the direction of Smolensk:

> We passed Mogilev, rolling towards our next target, Smolensk. The number 8 battery was a point unit and, on the way, we crossed a German 15cm battery that had been attacked and destroyed, though there was no trace of the enemy. The moon shone and our infantry benefited from it, advancing so quickly that we were soon completely isolated. The first vehicles of the column—the commander's car, the observation truck, and the vehicle carrying the general staff of the battery—had just passed a small hollow when a single shot fired from an antitank gun destroyed a prize of war that we were very interested in: a trailer containing 5,000 liters of fuel.

> We heard terrifying cries of "Hurrah!" from all sides, which unleashed a tempest of small-arms fire … we didn't need to be told what to do. Like a hedgehog spitting fire, we let off a barrage of shots and threw hand grenades like we were veterans of infantry combat.

They were soon relieved, as the rest of the artillery regiment had seen the gasoline tanker explode and marched immediately towards the fight.

Four Weeks at Yelnia

On July 22nd, the division advanced along the Minsk–Moscow road, but were forced to stop and reduce a Russian position established on a ridge east of Yelnia. This position was of key strategic importance, as the village was built at a crossroads just 300km from Moscow. Moreover, the high ground near Yelnia provided protection for the southeastern flank of Smolensk, so was a desirable asset for the invaders.

Despite a solid Russian defense and violent artillery fire, the Waffen-SS of the Deutschland Regiment reached the first crest of the first hill, the Der Führer Regiment following a little afterwards. However, this success did not come without loss. The next day, at 0600hrs, the Russians launched a counterattack. The fighting lasted the whole morning, but at 1200hrs, the Red Army was forced back to its start line. The Reich Division then received an order to go over to the defensive. Heid Rühl wrote:

> The Russians around Yelnia attacked with tanks and penetrated as far as our artillery positions. One of our stretcher-bearers was awarded an Iron Cross for destroying a Russian tank by throwing a grenade through its hatch. Done! The gunners finished by repelling the first armored attack, but it was renewed with more force and our motorcycle battalion was soon in trouble. We were subjected to rolling fire from artillery like we had never known before. The courage of our soldiers and the way they fought was made clear by the actions of the

A very strange scene: three naked Waffen-SS stormtroopers inspecting a destroyed Russian KV-1. (Rights reserved)

45

A Pz Kpfw T-34 747(r)-mod. 41 in SS Panzergrenadier Das Reich colours. The losses at Kharkov and Kursk were so heavy that numerous captured T-34s were put into service by the Germans.

In Profile:
Panzergrenadier Division Das Reich, Captured Vehicles

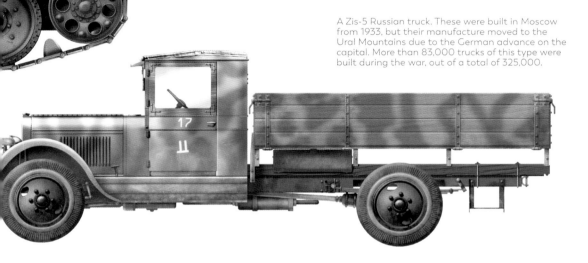

A Zis-5 Russian truck. These were built in Moscow from 1933, but their manufacture moved to the Ural Mountains due to the German advance on the capital. More than 83,000 trucks of this type were built during the war, out of a total of 325,000.

A Pz Kpfw T-34 KN 747(r). In a need for haste, this 1943 T-34 was not repainted. The Balkenkreuz has been added by hand, as has the Das Reich divisional insignia.

Russian soldiers let off steam with a wrestling match during a brief period of calm.

Kampfgruppe Förster, of the motorcycle battalion, who fought to the last man to stop the Soviets from getting through. With the help of the motorcyclists, we contained the enemy, but not for long as we started running out of ammunition. We were ordered to fire only on specific targets. Due to severe losses, the motorcycle battalion was withdrawn from the front and replaced by an engineering battalion from East Prussia.

The battle raged for several weeks. The SS Reich Division was temporarily withdrawn from the front line, but was soon back in action as the fighting redoubled in intensity on August 30th, when Zhukov launched a massive counterattack with the *24th Army, Stavka Strategic Reserves*. Seven Russian divisions were engaged, including the 102nd Armored Division.

The front was held by the 10th Panzer Division, the Reich Division and the 268th Infantry Division, with the support of the 202nd Assault Gun (Sturmgeschütz) Battalion.

This offensive occurred after more than a month of unremitting combat. For the first time since June 1941, the Russians had gone back on the attack, and after four days of fighting, the Germans were forced to retreat, abandoning Yelnia. It was the first German setback on the Eastern Front, but the 24th Russian Army could not follow it up and its losses were heavy—nearly 32,000 Soviet troops fell during the battle.

Opinions are divided over the results of this offensive: it seriously diminished the Soviet High Command (Stavka) reserves, but it was successful in stopping the Germans from racing to Moscow. It was also a clear warning to Hitler, who suddenly deprioritized Moscow as a target, deciding instead to focus on a better opportunity in the south, the Ukraine, whose economic value was considered much more important.

A look at the map told that both the 2nd and 1st Panzer Groups had advanced on either side far beyond the Soviets' stubborn group of armies holding on to Kiev on the Dnieper. All

A Soviet BA-10 armored car captured and reused by the Waffen-SS. The Germans captured large numbers of these during Operation *Barbarossa* and used them, among others, in the fight against the partisans. (Rights reserved)

Russian armorers inspect weapons—notably light mortars and an antiaircraft machine gun— in a tent during the summer or autumn of 1941. (Rights reserved)

Two Waffen-SS radio operators in 1941 or 1942. The insignia visible on the collar of the man in the headphones shows he belonged to the Wiking Division, which spent the entire war on the Eastern Front, unlike the Das Reich Division.

German soldiers in a Russian town. It often took several days to seize a town, during which period the fighting was of an extraordinarily violent nature.

Obergruppenführer Felix Steiner, former head of the Deutschland Regiment, became CO of the SS-Wiking. He is photographed here in the south of Russia in September 1942. (BA, Bild 101III-Moebius-139-08)

In Profile:
Felix Steiner

Along with Hausser, Felix Steiner was one of the military professionals who first forged the Waffen-SS into a formidable fighting force. As a young officer in the Great War Steiner had seen how skill and flexibility could overcome the bludgeoning attrition-tactics of firepower. When he took command of the SS-Deutschland Regiment he disdained drill and parades in favor of weapons-handling and close-combat skills.

After the French campaign Steiner was transferred from command in Das Reich to serve as head of the new Wiking Division. After SS-Wiking proved itself a stalwart in the Caucasus and in the chaotic aftermath of Stalingrad, Steiner was elevated again to corps command, and then put in charge of an *ad hoc* army group during the final defense of Berlin.

Today he is perhaps best known from transcripts of Hitler's last conferences in his underground bunker: "Where is Steiner?" the Führer kept asking. The fact is Steiner had refused to sacrifice his remaining men in a hopeless attack, and had instead directed them westward, to reach Anglo-American lines. Steiner survived the war and died in 1966.

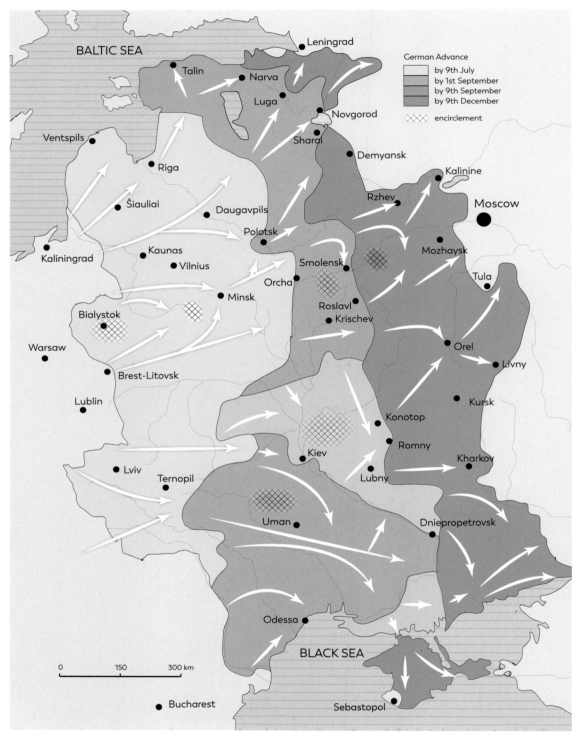

The stages of Operation Barbarossa, 1941. Note the series of encirclements on the road to Moscow, and then the largest one at Kiev, when Guderian's panzers drove south to join forces with Kleist's panzers driving north. Afterward Guderian, with the Reich Division, attacked toward Moscow, but could get only as far as Tula.

An SS Reich Division motorized column in Russia in September 1941. (BA, Bild 101III-Zschaeckel-130-05)

The Kiev Option

Hitler's decision to halt the drive on Moscow and instead divert Army Group Center's armor to the Ukraine (and Leningrad) has been debated ever since the war. Some consider it an early turning point, dooming Germany to failure in Russia, while others consider it his best move on the chessboard at the time.

Hitler himself, for lack of operational expertise, was imbued with history, and remembered that Napoleon had gone straight for Moscow, only to find himself isolated on an overstretched line, with the true strength of Russia swarming around him. Hitler needed economic resources, not simply the claim of a capital, and his destruction of the Kiev pocket opened up the Donetz industrial region plus a gateway to the Caucasus.

The big mistake may have been trying to take Moscow afterward, once the mud-season and winter were on their way. Exhausted German spearheads lost their supply lines, while the Soviets had fallen back on their own. If the Germans had simply consolidated their gains over the winter, then renewed their offensive in the spring, the story of Barbarossa may have ended differently.

A Sturmgeschütz III in its first incarnation, armed with a short 75mm cannon, towing a truck through a muddy pool in a Russian village. The arrival of autumn and its associated muddy conditions paralyzed the German operations. (BA, Bild 101I-140-1207-15)

Russian prisoners of war, most of whom are wounded, wait to be evacuated away from the front.
(Rights reserved)

that was needed was for the two panzer groups to join forces and the entire southern front in Russia could be surrounded and destroyed. This would allow German entrance to the Donetz industrial region, thence the Caucasus.

Withdrawn from the front for some rest and recuperation, the SS Reich Division subsequently took its place on the right flank of Guderian's attack behind the Kiev salient. The only worry was that the attack into the Ukraine was beginning as late as September. If not the Soviet armies, the Russian weather could not be held in abeyance for long.

Troubles in the Ukraine

On September 6th, the Reich's motorcycle battalion was tasked with seizing a bridge, intact, over the Desna, a tributary of the Dnieper, at Makoshyne. As it was strongly held by the Russians, the plan was to have a squadron of Stukas attacking before the SS soldiers, forcing the defenders to seek cover and allowing the SS to seize the bridge relatively unhindered.

For one reason or another, the planes were delayed, so General Guderian, commander of the armored group, ordered the SS motorcyclists to attack without support. This meant they would have to cross the bridge, atop Russian demolitions waiting to blow, and overcome the entrenchments on the other side.

The motorcyclists moved out. The machine-gunners, in sidecars, fired upon anything that moved. Somehow, they managed to seize the bridge and form a bridgehead on the far bank of the Desna, while engineers disarmed the explosives. It was only then that the Stukas arrived, following their original orders to plaster the far side of the river. The SS motorcycle battalion lost ten killed and some 30 wounded in this mistake—a common one on the rapidly expanding front.

During the following days, the division forged into Ukraine as the right flank of the panzer group until on September 14 Guderian's tanks joined hands with von Kleist's, from 1st Panzer Group, to seal off the Kiev pocket. More than 600,000 Russian soldiers were encircled and trapped in the cauldron, prompting the largest battlefield surrender in history to that time. Several Red Army divisions tried to hammer their way out of the ring, but these efforts generally ended up as bloodbaths. The students of the Kharkov military academy, for example, were totally annihilated when they renewed attacks against SS Reich Division machine-gunners.

Target Moscow

The victory at Kiev tore open the Soviets' southern front, allowing a German incursion into the Donetz industrial region and the Caucasus oil fields. But Hitler once again modified his plans, deciding now to advance against Moscow on the central front after all. He launched Operation *Typhoon* against Moscow at the beginning of the temporarily sunny and snow-free month of October 1941.

The new offensive began on October 4th for the Reich Division, which accompanied the 10th Panzer Division in the Vyazma sector. Soviet troops were soon trapped in a new pocket, but it was in front of Gzhatsk (now Gagarin) 58km northeast of Vyazma, that the Waffen-SS would embark upon an especially tough fight.

The Deutschland Regiment opened the divisional assault, reinforced by a squad of self-propelled StuG IIIs from the 3rd Battalion of the artillery regiment, augmented by a flak battery and an antitank company.

A stunning view of Red Square in Moscow, completely deserted following an explosion. (Rights reserved)

Winter uniforms were cruelly insufficient for war in extremely cold environments in 1942. Still, it was possible to paint helmets white for camouflage, leaving only the SS runes uncovered. (Rights reserved)

The 3rd Battalion began the attack at 0800hrs on October 7th followed by the 2nd Battalion at 1420hrs. Several villages were captured, one after the other. The 1st Battalion soon joined the fray, transported by trucks and advancing quickly when, suddenly, snow began to fall. It did not stick but quickly transformed the road into a quagmire, bogging down the trucks and rendering them useless. The troops were forced to continue on foot.

Despite this, the advance of the various battalions continued apace and the 3rd Battalion managed to cut the Smolensk–Moscow highway; the Russians were surrounded once more.

On October 9th, the Deutschland Regiment attacked Gzhatsk. The assault was rendered difficult by the intervention of Russian fighter-bombers plus snipers shooting down from the trees in a nearby forest that the Germans were forced to traverse on their way to the town. At 1300hrs, the 1st and 3rd Battalions arrived at Gzhatsk. The Russians had regrouped in the east, but despite intense fighting they could not retake the town. The German advance continued and by October 16th, they were just 3km from Yelnia. The first line of Russian defense had been eliminated.

Elsewhere, the Der Führer Regiment progressed along the road to Moscow, though with hard fighting, as on the way they ran into the 32nd Siberian Infantry Division, an elite

A train arrives from Germany loaded with new boots and warm clothing. The men attending the delivery are dressed irregularly; some of the lucky ones have managed to find furs. (BA, Bild 101I-287-892-10a)

unit specializing in hand-to-hand combat. Eventually overcoming the Siberians, finally, on October 18th, the Der Führer Regiment took the town of Mozhaysk. This did not seem to have a particularly damaging effect on the Russians.

A certain calm returned to the Reich Division as the troops could do no more and had to be relieved. In addition to the physical and mental combat exhaustion, many had fallen ill, due in no small part to the complete lack of appropriate winter uniforms.

On November 18th, the division returned to the front line, fighting alongside the 10th Panzer Division towards the Istra river. It took four days to take the village of Gorodishche. On the 25th, a bridgehead was established on the Istra. On the evening of the 26th, the town was taken, and a wedge firmly rammed into Moscow's internal defenses.

The final assault began on November 27th, in glacial temperatures. The advance was slow and difficult. The 2nd Battalion, Der Führer Regiment was virtually annihilated, its surviving troops distributed between the other two battalions. The same thing happened to the 3rd Battalion, Deutschland Regiment on December 1st. As to the 10th Panzer Division, it only had seven functioning tanks left.

Soon it was no longer possible to advance and commanders on the ground were demanding a retreat, at least for certain units. Hitler refused: everything the troops had taken had to be retained.

On December 4th, the 1st Company of the motorcycle battalion reached one of the termini of the Moscow tramway. The next day, the Soviet General Zhukov launched his huge counteroffensive.

German troops in retreat during the Russian offensive. The armored vehicle is a StuG III Ausf B, like those of the Reich Division.

The fighting on the Russian Front was of a severity never seen in the West, due mostly to the obstinacy of the Russian soldiers.

Russian troops with dogs, which are protected from snowfall by little white coats.

Siberian troops armed with an antitank PTRD-421 gun.

The body of a Waffen-SS stormtrooper outside Moscow. Despite his sheepskin jacket, the soldier's uniform is poorly adapted to the Russian winter.

The SS Reich Division in the Battle of Moscow

No less than 17 Russian armies were thrown into the battle—more than a million soldiers. The Soviet hammer fell on the Deutschland Regiment on December 6th at 0700hrs. Wave after wave, the assailants were mowed down by German machine-gunners. The front held until December 9th, when the army corps ordered a retreat, which did not please the SS. During the night of the 10th/11th, the division crossed the Istra towards the west, even as the front around the entire army corps was collapsing.

The retreat continued apace and, on January 16th, 1942, the division regrouped to the west of Gzhatsk. Defense frequently became offense when necessary or exigent as a matter of survival. The division took part in a counterattack near Rzhev and two Russian armies were surrounded, but it cost the motorcycle battalion four officers and 70 men on the first day of the attack—January 21st, 1942. Russian losses were even worse, their troops wiped out when they attempted to escape the murderous German ring. Otto Kumm, commander of the Der Führer Regiment, estimated that there were 15,000 bodies in front of his regiment, as well as 70 ruined Soviet tanks.

German losses were heavy too, and the self-propelled artillery unit was disbanded, as all its guns had been destroyed—its men were absorbed into the Der Führer Regiment. During the first week of February, a Russian offensive broke through on the divisional

German soldiers surrender to Russians during the Zhukov counteroffensive.

front, and Red Army tanks and infantry poured into the breach. The climax was reached on February 17th, when the Germans had to draw on the last of their reserves, service troops, and non-combat personnel to rescue the situation.

The Russians had to regroup, which gave the Germans time to do the same. When Obersturmbannführer Kumm returned to the divisional command post with his regiment, he met General Model, commander of the Ninth Army. Model announced that he was sending reinforcements to bring the regiment back to full strength.

Model then asked: "How strong is your regiment today?"

Kumm took Model to the window and said: "My entire regiment is outside, on the parade ground."

Model looked out the window where there were 35 men waiting in the snow. In June 1941, there had been 3,000.

Model was surely remembering this scene when, in 1943, he told Hitler—who was complaining that the German Army no longer had the state of mind it did in 1941—"The men of 1941 are all dead and buried in Russia."

By the end of February 1942, the SS Reich Division was no longer operational. It was hence transformed into the Kampfgruppe Reich. Little by little, however, reinforcements arrived, most of them from the Der Führer Regiment. The lightly wounded returned first, then a number of new recruits appeared, so that by the end of March the Kampfgruppe was able to return to the front to the west of Rzhev, on a bend of the Volga. The battle lasted about a month, with the Russians incapable of penetrating the front. However, the division needed to be entirely refitted and reorganized. On June 1st, 1942, it was relieved from the front and on the 10th, it arrived back in Germany. It had previously been named SS Das Reich

Division (mot.), but on November 9th, Hitler decided it was time to upgrade the division's armaments—and its name, which became the SS Panzergrenadier Division Das Reich.

The first consequence of this change was that the division received a panzer battalion equipped with Panzer IIIs and IVs, and that the 3d Battalion of the Der Führer Regiment became entirely armored, with SPW Sd Kfz 251 Hanomag half-tracks. The reconnaissance and motorcycle battalions were amalgamated into the SS Langemarck Regiment, equipped with amphibious Schwimmwagen vehicles.

At the beginning of July, the Der Führer Regiment was based at Le Mans, as the rest of the Das Reich Division began arriving in France. On November 11th, 1942, following the Allied landings in North Africa, the division occupied the French Free Zone and entered the enclosure of the Toulon arsenal on the 27th. This provoked the scuttling of the Toulon fleet, French Admiral Laborde having foreseen that any German incursion would necessitate the immediate destruction of every ship in the fleet.

By the end of the year, the SS Langemarck Regiment had been disbanded and its men redistributed between the reconnaissance and panzer battalions.

On January 15th, 1943, in light of the dramatic deterioration of the situation in Russia, the new SS Panzergrenadier Division Das Reich left again for the Eastern Front. It was not going to be a good year.

A Schwimmwagen in Russia. This one belongs to the Wehrmacht, but the Reich Division was also issued the vehicle when it became a panzergrenadier division. (Rights reserved)

The final phase of Operation *Lila*, the entry of the SS panzers into the Toulon naval base, did not go according to plan, as Admiral Laborde scuttled the entire French fleet. They didn't just sink the ships—they destroyed them completely so that the Germans would not be able to use them, which explains the explosions. (Top: BA, Bild 101I-620-2839-34a, Meinhold; Bottom: BA, Bild 101I-027-1451-10, Venneman Wolfgang)

Walter Model (left) and Heinz Guderian during Operation Barbarossa. At this time Model commanded the 3rd Panzer Division of Guderian's 2nd Panzer Group. Model is wearing the Knight's Cross that he earned when his division reached the Dnieper, on July 4th, 1941. During Operation *Typhoon*, Model commanded the XLI Panzer Corps. On December 5th, his 6th Panzer Division was just 22km from the Kremlin, but was unable to advance any further. (Rights reserved)

The aftermath of a winter battle on the Eastern Front, with Soviet small arms as well bodies littering the field. (Rights reserved)

In Profile:
Heinz Guderian

Germany's famous "Panzer Leader," Guderian, led the drive to the Channel during the Battle of France, and then commanded the 2nd Panzer Group of Army Group Center during the invasion of Russia. It was during Barbarossa that Guderian had SS-Reich under his command, and found he was able to give it critical tasks. During his drive to seal the Kiev Pocket, Guderian visited the division and wrote, "The excellent discipline of the troops made a first-class impression."

Guderian was made Chief of the German General Staff during the war's last year, his tenure marked by titanic arguments with Hitler, especially when Hitler determined to send 2nd SS Panzer and other top Waffen-SS divisions to Hungary in 1945, just as a Soviet juggernaut was about to descend on Berlin.

Guderian was held in US custody until 1948, but no charges were brought against him. He died in 1954 aged 65.

In Profile:
Walter Model

An experienced staff officer, Model began his storied combat career as head of the 3rd Panzer Division in Barbarossa, spearheading Guderian's drives on both Moscow and Kiev. Afterward he rose quickly to corps command, and then led Ninth Army through the crisis winter before Moscow.

His brusque, hands-on style of leadership made him "Hitler's fireman," as he seemed to specialize in retrieving impossible situations. When assigned to Normandy in August 1944, however, he bluntly told Hitler that the troops needed to retreat. He had become a rare Wehrmacht officer whose judgment Hitler trusted.

Model commanded Army Group B during the Ardennes Offensive and the following spring until, after a final defeat with the fall of the Ruhr, he walked off into a wood and shot himself.

A Marder on a Panzer 38 (t) chassis fighting in the streets of Kharkov at the end of winter 1943. In the foreground is the front of an Sd Kfz 251.

SS fighting technique

As the war went on, the Waffen-SS played an ever-larger role, especially after the crisis of the first Russian winter when SS formations proved like rocks. Instead of disdaining them, Army troops became drawn to them, and corps commanders came to see their value.

The Waffen-SS did have certain advantages, as most of its recruits were young, unmarried men, usually raised through the Hitler Youth system and imbued with diehard ideology. Beyond that, their patron, Himmler, ensured them the best and latest equipment. He could not spare them, however, from being put into battle wherever the fighting was thickest.

The 1943 Russian Campaign: Kharkov, Kursk, Back to Kiev

The disaster of the Sixth Army at Stalingrad and the penetration of the German front in southern Russia created a perilous situation for the Germans. Army Group A fighting in the Caucasus was in danger of being cut off. The breaches in the front were so large that the Stavka believed the war could be finished in this single campaign, if Soviet armies could only push onward to the Dnieper. The Germans' only remaining trump card was that Hitler–feeling a rare sense of humility after Stalingrad–had temporarily ceded operational control to Erich von Manstein, perhaps the only man able to reverse the calamity. Manstein immediately ordered 1st Panzer Army to withdraw from the Caucases and move to his left wing. He deployed the remnants of 4th Panzer Army as a screen in the steppes to protect the retreat through Rostov. Along the Don River, isolated German units were flung back and forth knocking out Soviet spearheads. Meantime reinforcements from the Reich were arriving, foremost among them the newly formed SS Panzer Corps–Leibstandarte, Das Reich, and Totenkopf Divisions–brought back to full strength. It was this cudgel, if properly employed, that could restore the entire German situation in Russia.

The SS divisions had recently been reformed and refitted, stronger than ever now with new recruits and the latest-model arms. They were now all Panzergrenadier divisions, with full armored complements, as can be seen in the table detailing the tanks in each division in February 1943:

SS Division Leibstandarte Adolf Hitler				
12 × Panzer II	10 × Panzer III lang*	52 × Panzer IV lang	9 × Tiger	9 × Panzerbefehl**
SS Division Das Reich				
10 × Panzer II	81 × Panzer III lang	21 × Panzer IV lang	10 × Tiger	9 × Panzerbefehl
SS Division Totenkopf				
71 × Panzer III lang	10 × Panzer III N	22 × Panzer IV lang	9 × Tiger	9 × Panzerbefehl

* *lang* (lit. long), denotes a longer, higher-powered barrel than its predecessor
** command tank

71

The following three photographs are from a little-known report on the tanks of the 2nd SS Panzer Regiment of the SS Panzergrenadier Division Das Reich on the Russian Front, during the winter of 1943.

A Tiger in the forest, the last in a column. The Tiger always impressed photographers from propaganda companies. (BA, Bild 101I-571-1721-31, Schnitzer)

Two Das Reich Panzer IVs are visible here, including one that has all its *schürzen* (protective skirts) in the foreground, and then a Tiger tank. (BA, Bild 101I-571-1721-26, Schnitzer)

Two Tigers of the 2nd SS Panzer Regiment. Note that they wear the same divisional insignia as during the Battle of Kursk. (BA, Bild 101I-571-1721-29, Schnitzer)

Heinz Harmel, commander of the 3rd Deutschland SS Panzergrenadier Regiment, on board an Sd Kfz 251 in September 1943. Beside him is an untersturmführer who is wearing a "Deutschland" armband. (BA, Bild 101III-Groenert-026-029)

The first unit that arrived in Russia was the 1st Battalion, Der Führer Regiment, which formed a kampfgruppe with a flak battery, two artillery batteries and the 14th Heavy Weapons Company. This battle group was put at the disposal of the 6th Panzer Division, and only rejoined Das Reich on March 7th, 1943.

Hitler gave precise orders: the SS armored corps would be used as a juggernaut of three divisions, flattening everything in its path. Things didn't quite work out that way, however, because as soon as a unit arrived at the front, it was thrown into battle where the need was greatest. By early 1943, all German positions in Russia were in a state of crisis, even though the Russian offensive was finally showing signs of weakness; its lines of supply and communication had been stretched to the limit. But Stalin refused to allow the offensive to falter as he felt the Germans were on the verge of total collapse.

The German commanders were willing to do anything to succeed, including the formation of kampfgruppen, which diluted the strike power of the divisions. At times there was no choice and, in the case of Das Reich, it was not the first time, as we have already seen.

Frozen bodies of German soldiers. The third Battle of
Kharkov took place in terrible conditions.
(Rights reserved)

July–August 1943 during Operation *Citadel* or its aftermath. The presence of the Panther in the Das Reich Division indicates that this photo was taken in August, as they did not have one at Kursk in July. They all belonged to the 39th Panzer Regiment. (BA Bild 101III-Merz-023-22)

Das Reich Under Threat

Das Reich had barely arrived at the front before it ran into difficulties. It took up defensive positions on the Oskol River, notably a bridgehead on the east bank, but Soviet pressure there was so strong that retreat was inevitable. On February 1st, the order was given to abandon the bridgehead. It was in the nick of time, as the Russians had already crossed the river and were streaming towards the Donets.

The reconnaissance battalion was separated from the bulk of the division, and it proved necessary to engage Das Reich's new armored regiment to retrieve the situation.

Soon, all eyes were turned to the town of Kharkov, towards which the Soviet armies were converging. It seemed that Stalin wanted to redress the German successes of spring 1942. Moreover, Kharkov was the Soviet Union's third largest city.

The Russian threat became clear, as the town was in danger of being caught in a pincer movement. To the south, the Soviets were driving a wedge into the flanks of the Leibstandarte Adolf Hitler to cut off its neighboring 320th Infantry Division. To the north, the Soviets had broken through, but the front had not as yet collapsed. It would either be necessary to abandon the city, or to throw the SS Panzer Corps into the fray, at the risk of its destruction.

On February 9th, the Das Reich Division withdrew, as its position was untenable. The passage was made in dreadful conditions—a blizzard—yet the Waffen-SS could not find shelter to the west of the river, because the Russians had already crossed it in several places. There was nothing left but to retreat again. The division then established a base just to the east of Kharkov, as an unwitting buffer against the Soviet thrust.

Paul Hausser, commander of the SS Panzer Corps, knew that he if he could not close the breach between the Leibstandarte Adolf Hitler and the 320th Infantry Division, the town would quickly fall. But how would this be possible when there were no tactical reserves to call upon? He would have to draw from the units already engaged, which would mean shortening the front.

In doing so, he succeeded in scraping together a kampfgruppe formed around the Der Führer Regiment and the Das Reich motorcycle battalion, which also included the "Panzer Mayer" motorcycle battalion of the Leibstandarte Adolf Hitler, and the Witt Regiment. This represented a greatly reduced force, but it was nonetheless solid enough. On February 10th, the kampfgruppe was ready. On that same day, Sturmbannführer Stadler replaced Gruppenführer Keppler, the victim of a brain hemorrhage, at the head of the Das Reich Division.

One of 90 Ferdinands distributed between the 653rd and 654th panzerjäger battalions during the Battle of Kursk. (Rights reserved)

Counterattack at Kharkov

The counterattack began on February 11th. It took the Russians by surprise, especially since it was triggered in a snow storm and came at them from behind. The Soviets had no time to react as the Germans surged through their ranks. The 7th Guards Cavalry Corps was crushed as the kampfgruppe continued its advance south, linking up with the 320th Infantry Division. The southern pincer of the Red Army was therefore cut off and the threat against Kharkov from this direction was removed. The kampfgruppe was then disbanded and the troops rejoined their original units.

However, the situation had not improved to the east of the city. The Red Army assaults consisted of wave upon wave of infantry but with little artillery support as ammunition had run out. Soviet losses were colossal, especially since the Waffen-SS had received a new machine gun, the MG-42, with a rate of fire double that of the MG-34.

Nevertheless, the German defense slowly eroded. The destruction of the Russian southern pincer had not discouraged the Stavka—indeed, it had the opposite effect. The town of Belgorod, to the northeast, had just been retaken and these victorious Soviet divisions were now turning their considerable power toward Kharkov. What could the SS armored corps do? According to Hitler's orders, they were under no circumstances to retreat, but SS Panzer Corps commander General Paul Hausser was eventually forced to disobey the Führer, and gave the order to abandon Kharkov. The Germans left the city on February 15th, 1943.

Three officers of the Waffen-SS in a car, autumn 1943: SS Sturmbannführer Karl Ulrich, 6th SS Panzergrenadier Regiment Theodor Eicke; SS Sturmbannführer Anton Laackmann, 3rd Panzer Division Totenkopf; and SS Sturmbannführer Georg Bochmann, 2nd Panzer Division Das Reich. (BA, Bild 101III-Adendorf-131-22)

BA, Bild 183-H01758/o.Ang.

In Profile: Erich von Manstein

A Prussian born in 1877, von Manstein served throughout the Great War, and at the start of World War II was chief of staff of Rundstedt's Army Group. It was he who devised the plan that toppled France in 1940, and at the start of Barbarossa he commanded a panzer corps. Elevated to command of Eleventh Army, he conquered the Crimea in 1942, and then turned back a Soviet counteroffensive at Leningrad.

Later that year he was named commander of Army Group Don to retrieve the German calamity at Stalingrad, which he miraculously did, in part, by directing the SS Panzer Corps into its counteroffensive toward Kharkov. That summer he led Army Group South's wing of the Kursk offensive, again using the Waffen-SS as a spearhead, and believed that in history's greatest tank battle victory was at hand. Hitler was

distracted by the Allied invasion of Sicily, however, and called off the battle.

Through the rest of the year and into 1944 Manstein guided the Germans' strategic retreat, arguing with Hitler all the while to cede ground in favor of gaining operational reserves. Hermann Balck, considered by some the best tactical commander of the war, reflected in his memoir on the constant arguments between Hitler and his most brilliant commander. "Manstein could have been our savior," he wrote, "but that was what Hitler himself wanted to be."

In the end Hitler committed suicide once the Russians had overrun Berlin, while Manstein went on to write his post-war memoir, called "Lost Victories," before passing away in 1973.

The retreat was not easy as the Russian attacks were relentless, but Das Reich resisted with bloody consequences for the Red Army, leaving the ashes of mountainous Russian food and ammunition depots in its wake.

Manstein Plans a Counteroffensive

When General Hausser disobeyed Hitler, he never imagined that retreating from Kharkov would mean abandoning it completely. Von Manstein, commander of Army Group South, was of the same opinion. But first he had to destroy the most dangerous Russian armies, those marching on Dnipropetrovsk.

The battle took place between the Dnieper and the Donets from February 19th to March 4th, 1943. The Das Reich Division was the first into action, followed by the Totenkopf Division. On the 24th, the Germans seized Pavlograd: it was an easy victory, relatively speaking, and the Soviets retreated eastward. However, this was not enough to put a stop

Russian infantry advance under the protection of an SU 76 self-propelled gun in autumn 1943. (Rights reserved)

Das Reich Tigers deployed during the Battle of Kursk in July 1943. (BA, Bild 101III-Zschaeckel-206-34)

A Sturmgeschütz flipped by an explosion during the Battle of Kursk.

A column of Das Reich Tigers on their way to participate in Operation *Citadel*, June 1943. (BA, Bild 101III-Zschaeckel-207-12)

to the Russian assaults, as the Stavka seemed to have infinite resources at its disposal. Soon the 1st Army, Popov's armored corps and several motorized corps entered the fray. The eight days of fighting that followed were horrifically violent but, at their conclusion, the Russians were once again forced to retreat 120km over a wide front of 100km.

The tables had turned. From the beginning of February, the Germans were seeing more successes on the battlefield, particularly on the Donets—more than 100,000 Russian soldiers had been neutralized south of the river. Meanwhile, the Waffen-SS was getting closer to Kharkov. On March 10th two kampfgruppen launched an assault: to the west of the town, the 3rd Battalion of the Deutschland Regiment, accompanied by a tank battalion from the Totenkopf prepared to enter Kharkov, while a Der Führer kampfgruppe provided cover. On March 11th, the troops entered the town, but the Russian resistance was almost fanatical in its ferocity. Within three days, the Red Army had lost its 1st and 2nd Guards Tank Corps, as well as four infantry divisions. On March 15th, Kharkov was once again in German hands.

The huge success at Kharkov put an end to the Red Army's winter offensive, leaving the front uneven and unstable, particularly in the central sector where there remained a deep Russian salient into the German front around Kursk. For the Germans, this "protrusion" would be their next target on the Eastern Front.

Kursk: Hitler's Signal

For Hitler, the Germans' 1943 summer offensive was an absolute necessity, and not only to retake the initiative in the East, lost since Operation *Uranus* in November 1942, and the capitulation of the Sixth Army at Stalingrad in February 1943. It would also be a warning to the whole world: Germany once more had the means to win.

The German plan wasn't exactly original, as it was clear to both sides that the Wehrmacht would next attack the salient at Kursk: the Russians could therefore prepare for the assault.

The plan for Operation *Citadel* was to cut the salient off at its base by attacking from two directions: the Ninth Army and three armored corps from the north, and from the south, the Fourth Panzer Army with three panzer corps, including the SS Panzer Corps, now designated "II," though still composed of the Leibstandarte Adolf Hitler, Das Reich and Totenkopf divisions.

The Russian plan was rather more complex: they weren't just going to repel the German offensive, but would launch their own quasi-general offensive, allowing the enemy no respite.

For Operation *Citadel*, Das Reich had been refitted and reinforced. It now had:

- 1 × Panzer II
- 62 × Panzer III lang
- 33 × Panzer IV lang
- 14 × Tiger
- 25 × T-34 (captured)
- 10 × Panzerbefehl

The other SS divisions were similarly equipped.

Operation *Citadel*

The offensive began on July 5th, 1943. Contrary to what the Stavka had believed, the Germans' principal effort was in the south of the salient, rather than the north, which forced it to quickly transfer troops from one sector of the front to another.

On the II SS Panzer Corps front, it was the Leibstandarte Adolf and Das Reich divisions that attacked first, the Totenkopf being kept in reserve to exploit any perceived success. But even before the troops crossed their start lines, they were hit with a barrage of Russian artillery fire, which caused widespread damage and confusion.

The German advance was extremely slow, due to the sheer number of Russian defensive lines. The grenadiers had to battle all day for very little gain. It was only on the Leibstandarte's front that the armored regiment broke through to the second line of defense, near the village of Yakovleva.

In Profile:
The 2nd SS Panzergrenadier Division Das Reich at Kursk

A Ford V3000S of the 2nd SS Panzer Regiment Das Reich. These Fords were manufactured at the Niehl factory, Cologne. This version first appeared in 1941.

The Germans owed their early success in the war to the agility and power of their panzer arm; however, upon encountering the Soviet T-34 at the height of *Barbarossa*, German designers had to rush back to their drawing boards. The result was the Panther, which unfortunately suffered many teething pains, and the Tiger, which soon became king of the jungle. Though not highly mobile, and susceptible to breakdowns, the Tiger in its final form became the most feared weapon of the war.

A Tiger I Ausf H1 of the 2nd Panzer Regiment at Kursk. Tigers were assigned to each of the SS divisions that made up the SS Panzer Corps. Later, they would be reunited within the 102nd SS Panzer Battalion.

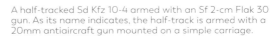

A half-tracked Sd Kfz 10-4 armed with an Sf 2-cm Flak 30 gun. As its name indicates, the half-track is armed with a 20mm antiaircraft gun mounted on a simple carriage.

The next day, the Der Führer Regiment passed through the Deutschland Regiment to renew the assault, and this time made significant progress, at least until a barrage of artillery fire interrupted the troops' momentum. It took severe retaliation from the German artillery to move ahead. Hill 243 fell, and with it the path to Prokhorovka. This threatened the entire southern front of the Kursk salient, so the Stavka sent in large numbers of armored units to prop up the sector. Luftwaffe Stukas, fitted with new antitank guns, were brought in to fight them off, but it was not enough to halt the Russian counterattacks. SS Panzergrenadier Division Das Reich was forced onto the defensive after only three days of combat: it quickly became clear that the German offensive had not started off as well as had been hoped.

On July 8th, Russian armored attacks increased in volume and intensity, relentlessly so. By 1330hrs, the Deutschland Regiment had already repelled three such attacks. In all, on the SS Panzer Corps front, the Germans destroyed 290 Russian tanks, essentially due to the efforts of the panzer regiment Das Reich.

On July 9th, the Soviet 1st Tank Corps attempted to surround the II SS Panzer Corps, which was itself trying to do the same to them. The Das Reich Division held the eastern

Two Panzer IIs: one damaged, the other in flames. This Russian photograph apparently dates to the Battle of Kursk, though the Panzer II would have been a rare sight at that time. (Rights reserved)

A typical view of the Battle of Kursk: two Waffen-SS stormtroopers in the grass watching the enemy lines. The terrain is completely flat, which does not lend itself to the German style of armored warfare; panzers can be easily detected by entrenched Russian antitank gun batteries. (Rights reserved)

flank, while the other two divisions tried to progress towards Prokhorovka. Das Reich was subjected to numerous counterattacks until July 11th.

On July 12th, Fourth Panzer Army renewed its efforts against Prokhorovka, setting the stage for the largest tank battle in history. Some suggest the number of Panzers employed as 600, which could be true if one considers the earlier table, but after more than a week of intense fighting, it seems unrealistic that so many tanks would still be available and functioning. On the Russian side, the 5th Guards Tank Army had around 859 tanks available.

In a rare case of a frontal attack by both sides, the battle that ensued was effectively an attempt by each side to annihilate his adversary. It was chaotic, and quickly disintegrated into a series of separate, smaller engagements. By the end of the day the Germans held the field, among hundreds of smoldering tanks, most of them Russian—but a decisive breakthrough had not been accomplished.

A rare shot of a 39th Panzer Regiment tank destroyed during the Battle of Kursk. Russian machine-gunners have set up their gun alongside the remains of the turret. (Rights reserved)

April 1943 in the Kharkov sector. Reichsführer Heinrich Himmler inspects a company of Tigers from the Das Reich Division. (BA, Bild 101III-Zschaeckel-198-28)

Another typical scene from the Battle of Kursk. An Sd Kfz. 250/11 equipped with a 2.8cm sPzB 41 antitank gun. (NARA)

The next day, General Hermann Hoth directed the Das Reich Division, which had held the right flank the previous day, to renew the attack. July 13th was not a good day for the Germans: to the north of the salient, Model's Ninth Army was brought to a standstill as the Second Panzer Army, which had been on its left, was subjected to a massive attack that threatened Model's rear. Hoth's Fourth Panzer Army was therefore forced to continue the fight alone. Meantime, far from Kursk, in the Mediterranean, the British and Americans were landing in Sicily.

On July 14th, the SS Panzergrenadier Division Das Reich launched its assault. It initially made good progress, capturing a village after a savage fight, advancing further without interruption, and destroying several Russian tanks for good measure. But for all that, no decisive breakthrough was made, and after nine days of fighting it was becoming clear that Operation *Citadel* would not achieve its goals: there were still 130km to cover to reach the nearest of the Ninth Army troops in the north of the Kursk salient. It was an impossible task.

Hitler suspended the operation under the pretext of needing troops to send to the Mediterranean. He authorized the continuation of assaults south of Kursk, but only on the condition that the SS Panzer Corps would not participate—they were destined for Italy. The three SS divisions were therefore withdrawn from the front, superficially reorganized, and prepared for departure by long-distance train. However, the Russians were setting their own plans in motion, and began attacking to the north of the Kursk salient as well as in the south.

A Tiger of the Das Reich division in the Kharkov sector, April 1943. (BA, Bild 101III-Gutscher-001-03)

The Fourth Battle of Kharkov

The situation quickly became perilous, especially in the south, as the Red Army once again threatened Kharkov. On August 4th, Army Detachment Kempf, under whose command we now find the Das Reich Division, received a message from Army Group South:

> An order from the Führer has placed the Das Reich Division under the command of Army Group South and it must concentrate in the sector of Kharkov. All preparations made by the division for an eventual transfer to Italy must be halted immediately.

In the end, only the Leibstandarte Adolf Hitler left for the Mediterranean. Before doing so, it transferred all its armored vehicles to Das Reich. A new armored corps was formed: the

The Resilience of the Red Army

One of the remarkable factors of World War II is how the Soviet armed forces, despite suffering calamity after calamity, managed to continue to grow and strengthen throughout the war, until they finally overwhelmed the most professional military machine of modern times.

Part of it was having territory to spare, as well as an ally in brutal weather, which historically punished Western invaders diving too far into Russian depths. Another part was assistance from the Anglo-Americans, who, while devastating German industry through airpower, passed a constant stream of supply to the Soviets through Murmansk and Iran. Millions of tons of weaponry, plus transport and raw materials, were passed to the Russians to compensate for their own loss of industrial plant.

The Red Army also gained expertise and skill after its many battles with the Germans, though in the end it was the pure determination of their people in defense of the Motherland that turned the tide. The Soviets, far and away, suffered the most casualties of any combatant in World War II.

July 1943, during the Battle of Kursk. The grenadiers of an SS division (either Totenkopf or Das Reich) accompany a group of tanks in their Sd Kfz 251. (Rights reserved)

In Profile:
Panzer III and StuG III

While German designers, including Porsche, fiddled with how brilliant to make new Panthers and Tigers, earlier engineers had created a workhorse in the Panzer III that would prove valuable throughout the war. Provided with flexibility in its gun-mount, the Panzer III could be upgraded from a 37mm cannon to a long-barreled 50mm, once T-34s were encountered.

Meantime its chassis lent itself to a self-propelled gun called the Sturmgeschütz (StuG) III, which would become the most numerous Wehrmacht armored vehicle. Without a revolving turret but with a more powerful cannon (75mm), the StuG was both a superb defensive weapon and cheaper to produce. Its low profile made for a difficult enemy target, while its official status as (SP) artillery allowed it to be sprinkled among infantry as well as panzer divisions.

The Sturmgeschütz III Bismarck of the 2nd Panzergrenadier Division Das Reich at Kharkov, April 1943. It is sand-green, and its name is painted over the Balkenkreuz.

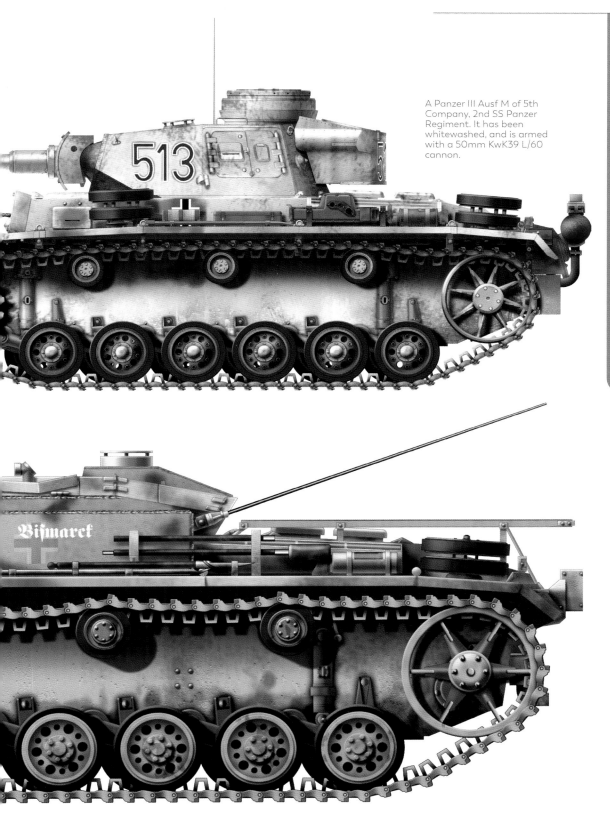

A Panzer III Ausf M of 5th Company, 2nd SS Panzer Regiment. It has been whitewashed, and is armed with a 50mm KwK39 L/60 cannon.

July 1943, the Battle of Kursk. The crew of a Panzer III, from the 2nd SS Panzer Regiment take a brief rest behind their tank as the battle rages ahead of them. (BA Bild 101III-Zschaeckel-208-25)

III Panzer Corps, which included the Das Reich and Totenkopf divisions, along with the Army's 3rd Panzer Division. The corps was directed towards the Mius river to protect the flank south of Kharkov and to re-establish contact with the Fourth Panzer Army. This was achieved at the beginning of August, but the success was short-lived.

On August 18th, the Red Army launched its final offensive to liberate Kharkov. The 53rd Army struck in the north, as did the 57th, while the remains of the 5th Guards Tank Army prepared to deliver the coup de grâce.

The offensive was initially stopped in its tracks, exactly as the Germans had been a month earlier at Kursk. On Das Reich's defensive front, Soviet losses were particularly heavy: on August 19th alone no less than 184 tanks were destroyed.

The Russians, however, were not discouraged, and on August 22nd, they broke through in another sector. The Der Führer Regiment was called upon to help, but it was not enough to reverse the damage, Manstein resolved to evacuate Kharkov, despite Hitler's orders to the contrary. He later said: "I would rather lose a town than the six divisions defending it." The truth was that Soviet pressure was so unrelenting and there would be no second miracle at Kharkov. On September 15th, the Army Group Command gave the order to retreat to the Dnieper.

During the difficult winter battles that followed, the Das Reich Division was once again reduced to the effective strength of a kampfgruppe, with two armored companies and a battalion each from the Deutschland and Der Führer regiments.

This kampfgruppe had the misfortune of staying on the Eastern Front until April 8th, 1944, when it was placed in reserve before departing a week later for Toulouse. This concluded the second campaign of the Das Reich Division on the Eastern Front, but it was a case of out of the frying pan and into the fire for the stormtroopers, who would next be on their way to Normandy.

The Two-Front War

After the expulsion of the British Army at Dunkirk in June 1940, followed by the surrender of France, Nazi Germany had a full four years to achieve a decisive outcome against the Soviet Union before it would again have to face the Western allies in France.

With the failure of *Barbarossa* in 1941, and the worse disaster at Stalingrad in 1942, followed by the climatic, but drawn battle of Kursk in 1943, time had run out. In the East all hope of toppling the Soviets was gone and the Germans had switched to a defensive strategy.

In the West, however, there was still confidence that battle-hardened German divisions could obliterate the less tested Anglo-Americans once they invaded the northern continent. For this reason, SS-Das Reich, now a full panzer division, as well as the Leibstandarte, Hitlerjugend, and other Waffen-SS formations would be thrown against the Allied invasion front. It would be a test between massive Allied power and German combat expertise in 1944, with the fate of Europe hanging in the balance.

From left to right, Walter Krüger, Heinrich Himmler and Paul Hausser at Kharkov in April 1943. (BA Bild 101III-Zschaeckel-198-19/Zschaeckel.)

In Profile:
Commanders of Das Reich

From September 1939 to May 1945, SS-Das Reich was led by no fewer than 15 different divisional commanders. This is aside from officers within the ranks, such as Felix Steiner, who were elevated from regimental command to take over other divisions, or even armies, as the war progressed.

The division's first commander, Paul Hausser, went on to lead Seventh Army in Normandy, although his finest hour may have been when he defied Hitler's order to hold Kharkov in March 1943. Instead he refused to repeat Stalingrad and saved his corps, recapturing the city on his own (and Manstein's) initiative.

Wilhelm Bittrich went on to lead the II SS-Panzer Corps during *Market Garden*, while Matthias Kleinheisterkamp took control of SS-Nord and later led several late-war corps. Walter Kruger similarly went on to corps command, after leading Das Reich in 1943, adding the Oak Leaves and Swords to his Knights Cross. Kruger was among a number of German commanders, like Model, who committed suicide at the end, rather than witness his cause lost.

The shortest tenure of a Das Reich commander was that of Christian Tychsen, a highly decorated young colonel in the East, who was named commander of the division when Heinz Lammerding was invalided during Operation *Cobra* in Normandy. Tychsen lasted only four days in command, as he was ambushed by US 2nd Armored troops while on his way to assume control.

Throughout the war, the men of Das Reich remained unfamiliar with the concept of a "rear-area" commander.

During the Battle of Kursk, Russian infantrymen approach several destroyed Panzer IIIs. The leader is armed with a PTRD 41 antitank gun, while the other has a PPsh 41 submachine gun. (Rights reserved)

In April 1943, after the third Battle of Kharkov, men of the Das Reich Division parade in front of their commander, SS Obergruppenführer Walter Krüger, who is standing on a Tiger, before a Knight's Cross presentation. In the background is an Sd Kfz 7 armed with a Flakvierling flak gun. (BA, Bild 101III-Zschaeckel-197-09)

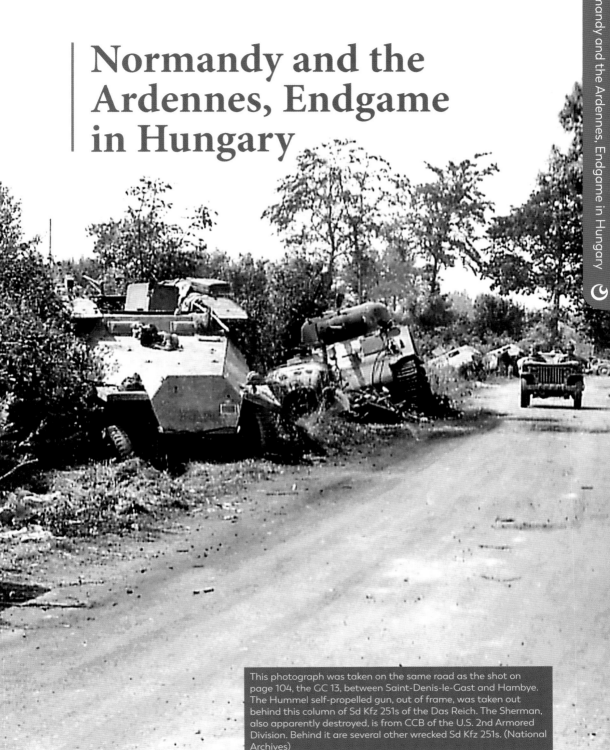

Normandy and the Ardennes, Endgame in Hungary

This photograph was taken on the same road as the shot on page 104, the GC 13, between Saint-Denis-le-Gast and Hambye. The Hummel self-propelled gun, out of frame, was taken out behind this column of Sd Kfz 251s of the Das Reich. The Sherman, also apparently destroyed, is from CCB of the U.S. 2nd Armored Division. Behind it are several other wrecked Sd Kfz 251s. (National Archives)

With the return of its kampfgruppe from the Eastern Front, the Das Reich Division was once more complete, though again it needed to absorb thousands of new personnel to replace casualties. For the first time, it had the status of panzer division, and as such it had top-notch equipment. It was based in the southwest of France, not to recover, but to serve as a strategic reserve for the OKW, which was well aware that the Allies would attempt to land in France in 1944.

Numbers of tanks in the 2nd SS Panzer Division Das Reich in June 1944 were as follows:

- 13 × Stug III
- 78 × Panzer IV lang
- 79 × Panther
- 12 × Flakpanzer 38, armed with 3.7cm antiaircraft guns

It had, therefore, the complete 1944 theoretical strength of a model panzer division.

D-Day

On June 6th, at news of the Allied invasion, the Das Reich Division was put on alert and its wheeled armored elements departed for Normandy the same evening. It was more difficult for the tanks, as they needed to be transported by train. Embarkation was to have taken place at Montauban but the station had been bombed by aircraft. The first train arrived at the Loire on June 11th, but the few bridges spanning it had been damaged. The tanks had to wait until June 23rd to eventually join the rest of the division on the battlefield.

In the meantime, the invasion had prompted a widespread uprising of the French Resistance, and Das Reich found itself in running fights with armed members of the Maquis. Some elements committed a series of war crimes, notably at Tulle and at Oradour-sur-Glane, the latter a pure reprisal against civilians. These tragedies were inexcusable and it is certain that some troops adopted in France the same scorched-earth conduct used in Russia where massacring civilians and razing villages to the ground was commonplace. The German Army itself, including Rommel, was horrified by the news of Oradour and demanded an investigation. However, the commander on the scene, Adolf Diekmann, was shortly after killed on the invasion front, along with much of his battalion, so the true inquiry only came after the war.

The Das Reich Division did not particularly distinguish itself in Normandy, as it was once more divided up into different kampfgruppen attached to other divisions—particularly the 9th SS Panzer Division Hohenstaufen—thus making it less effective as a unit. After having fought against the British and Canadian sectors in June, for example, during Operation *Epsom*, the various kampfgruppen disbanded, and the division was transferred to face the American sector near the Cotentin peninsula on July 4th. There, the division was again split into kampfgruppen to support various infantry divisions. One of these units, Kampfgruppe Weldinger, was assigned to the 353rd Infantry Division.

Dradour, a village near Limoges, following the massacre of over 600 of its inhabitants by a battalion of the Das Reich Division. (National Archives)

A villager walks past an annihilated German column in front of the church at Roncey, which was itself totally destroyed by air raids. The first vehicle in this shot cannot be identified, but the others—which were possibly destroyed by their own crews—are Marder IIIs. (National Archives)

In Profile:
The Das Reich in Normandy

An Sd Kfz 251-9 Ausf D of Kampfgruppe Lamerding during the battle for Normandy.

An Sd Kfz 234 Puma of the reconnaissance battalion, Das Reich Division. The camouflage with foliage was often used to hide vehicles from Allied aircraft.

An Sd Kfz 162 Hummel of the 2nd SS Panzer Artillery Regiment. Several armored vehicles of this type were lost in the Roncey Pocket.

In Normandy, commanders from the East who had only faced the Soviet Air Force were surprised by the massive superiority of Anglo-American airpower, though Western commanders such as Field Marshal Rommel tried to warn them.

With the Luftwaffe overmatched, the Germans' only recourse on the ground was to camouflage their vehicles, either through design or with foliage. Major movements had to be restricted to night, or bad weather, to avoid the ubiquitous "Jabos" plastering the roads. Another recourse was to close tightly with Allied attackers, abetted by Normandy's labyrinth of hedgerows, so that enemy aircraft would be fearful of hitting their own men.

103

An emblematic photograph of the Roncey Pocket: the remains of two armored vehicles from the 2nd SS Panzer Division are inspected by American soldiers following the battle. The scene took place on July 31st, 1944, in the Saint-Denis-le-Gast sector. In the foreground, the Sd Kfz 251 Ausf D wears the tactical symbol of the 1st tracked battery of an artillery regiment. In front of this, the "Clausewitz" is a Hummel belonging to the 1st Battalion, 2nd SS Panzer Artillery Regiment. (National Archives)

At first, it is difficult to distinguish what lies among the ruins of the church at Roncey. On closer inspection, however, it becomes clear that it is an Sd Kfz 7 with an armored cabin. Behind it is the tube of a 37mm Flak cannon, which may have been mounted on the vehicle. The number 122 is painted on the flank of one of the Marder IIIs destroyed in front of the church. (National Archives)

On July 8th, the US 3rd Armored Division was stopped in its tracks when it attempted to break through the German lines. This was partly thanks to the mammoth solo efforts of Unterscharführer Ernst Barkmann, a Waffen-SS tank commander who survived the war and died in 2009.

Operation *Cobra*: Subsequent Breakout

After the American breakthrough on July 25th, west of Saint-Lô, the German command was caught out, as the breach in the line could not be plugged. The front in the American sector had been cut in two. Paul Hausser who now commanded Seventh Army, could see no way to reconstruct the line south of Coutances, so he ordered the units situated west of the American breakthrough to themselves break out towards the southeast, where the bulk of the German forces could be found.

The situation on July 27th was as follows: the troops isolated south of Coutances could retreat farther south without encountering any Americans, as long as they acted quickly. However, if they obeyed Hausser's order to advance southeast, they would have to break through American armored divisions. But even before Field Marshal von Kluge overruled Hausser's order, the first pockets of Americans had already formed around the village of Roncey. More than 5,000 German troops were captured trying to break through to the southeast, while some escaped southward before the Americans arrived.

A One-Day Pocket

The existence of the Roncey Pocket was ephemeral, to say the least: it lasted for less than 48 hours, starting at around midnight on July 27th, when US Combat Command B (CCB), 2nd Armored Division took Notre-Dame-de-Cenilly unopposed, 20km south of the German line, which was largely to the north of Coutances. It seemed that nothing could stop the Americans, as all that lay before them now were the shattered remains of the Panzer Lehr Division and the 275th Infantry Division. The combat-ready German elements were far from Roncey—to the east, the vanguard of 2nd Panzer Division was at Tessy-sur-Vire, 15km away, while the advance troops of the 17th SS Panzergrenadier Division were digging in at Coutances, 12km away. If the Americans had been of a mind, they could have reached the sea at Bréhal by July 28th, surrounding six German divisions:

- 2nd SS Panzer Division Das Reich

- 17th SS Panzergrenadier Division Götz von Berlichingen

- 5th Fallschirmjäger Division

- 243rd Infantry Division

- 91st Air Landing Division

- 353rd Infantry Division

However, CCB, despite its strength, would not have been able to hold the extended front from Notre-Dame-de-Cenilly to Bréhal alone. Furthermore, it received orders to go no further than Lengronne, to establish roadblocks on all the roads coming from the north, and to hold all the bridges in the area, particularly those over the Sienne. The farthest advanced elements were therefore sent to seize the bridges during the night, while those situated too far ahead had to be blown up. 2nd Armored's CCB fulfilled its mission as far as Cerences, with just one bridge at Gavray escaping seizure or destruction due to German resistance. At Lengronne, a small task force comprising a company of tanks and a company of infantry tried to hold the strategically important crossroads between Coutances and Gavray, but they were not strong enough to prevent the determined Germans from passing. This was particularly the case for several German tanks heading towards Saint-Denis-le-Gast, which belonged either to the 2nd or the 17th SS.

On the morning of July 28th, German units began arriving at Saint-Denis-le-Gast in force. The 17th SS Panzergrenadier Division was covering the Mont Pinçon and Cerisy-la-Salle sector, with the Panther battalion of 2nd SS Panzer on its right. The rest of the units, which mostly belonged to the 275th Infantry Division, were concentrated around the Panthers. On the morning of the 28th, these elements assaulted the 183rd Field Artillery Battalion, an organic unit of the US VII Corps supporting the 2nd Armored Division. CCB's lines were soon cut, but were quickly restored by the Divisional Reserve of the 2nd Armored. This effort, however, allowed large numbers of Germans to escape. For the Americans, this clash meant that several German divisions farther north might now be surrounded, so the CCB turned its attention in that direction.

In the pocket it was chaos, as the German units were breaking out in the worst possible conditions, with no communications between themselves or with command. During the day Allied fighter-bombers plastered anything they could see on the roads, forcing the Germans into forests and ensuring they could only move at night. In the general confusion and probably due to the lack of communications, Obersturmführer Christian Tychsen, temporary commander of the 2nd SS Panzer Division found himself near Gavray in his Kübelwagen, nose-to-nose with an American tank. In the fight that followed he was fatally wounded, and despite being helped by the Americans he died soon afterwards and was buried in the German cemetery at Marigny. He was replaced as commander by Otto Baum.

Confusion on the Ground

Baum, the new head of Das Reich, did not exactly comply with Hausser's orders to break through the American line. Instead, he ordered his troops to retreat south of the Sienne, then make their way towards Percy, avoiding the American defenses altogether. However, not all of the troops received the message, and many units regrouped around Roncey with the intention of breaking out towards the southeast. These included not only units from

Carcasses at Roncey. To the right of the church steps is a Marder; the wreck on the left is that of a Schwimmwagen. Curiously, the houses beside the church do not appear to have been damaged at all—even their windows are intact. On the armor plating in front of the steps, you can make out a registration bearing the letters WH, which implies that the vehicle came from the Wehrmacht and did not belong to the Waffen-SS. (National Archives)

the 2nd SS Panzer Division but the engineering battalion and other elements of the 17th SS Panzer Division, and the bulk of the 6th Fallschirmjäger Regiment.

A little before dawn on July 29th, an *ad hoc* kampfgruppe with an 88mm self-propelled gun in the van, according to American sources, fell on the American defenders at a crossroads 5km southwest of Notre-Dame-de-Cenilly, where it was met by a company of tanks and a company of infantry. The American line was nearly broken before the SP gun team was killed, which halted the German advance. The Americans counted 17 enemy dead, plus 150 wounded, having themselves lost 50 men, a tank and a half-truck. No one knows how many Germans managed to sneak away on foot during the night.

Meanwhile, a little farther afield, 15 German tanks and several hundred men overwhelmed the position of a company from the US 4th Infantry Division, which had recently arrived in the area. The Germans then encountered CCB's artillery, reinforced by four guns from the 702nd Tank Destroyer Battalion. The fighting was extremely violent with seven Panzer IVs knocked out and 125 German dead. Fights such as this were playing out across the whole of Normandy through the night. While the Germans were often able to escape, they were usually forced to abandon their vehicles.

In Profile:
The Das Reich in 1945

A Panzer IV Ausf H of the 6th Company of the 2nd SS Panzer Regiment in Hungary in 1945. The gun barrel has been replaced due to wear.

+631

Hungary tanks

Incredibly, German military-industrial production reached a peak in autumn 1944, and its weapon designs were superior to any opponents'. However, Allied strategic bombing, plus loss of territory, inexorably reduced the Reich's resources, especially its supply of fuel.

In March 1945 Hitler launched his last offensive of the war, including SS-Das Reich and other Waffen-SS divisions, to safeguard his few remaining oil fields. The failure of this campaign in Hungary spelled final doom to the regime.

A Jagdpanzer 38 Hetzer of the 2nd SS Panzer Division in Bohemia in 1945. This type of tank hunter was prevalent at the end of the war due to ease of construction and reliability.

An Sd Kfz 251-1 Ausf D of the Das Reich Division in Bohemia in 1945. This was the most common model, used to transport troops. A Panzerschreck antitank rocket launcher is attached to the armored flank.

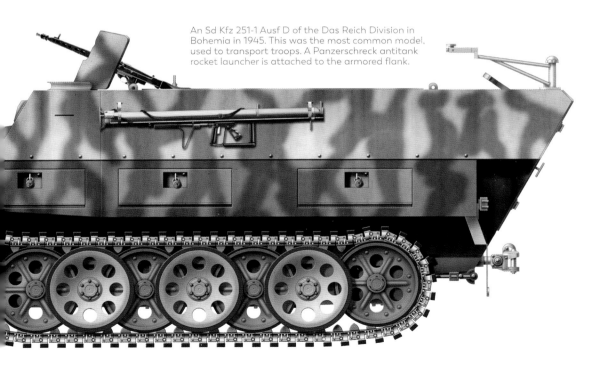

This photograph was taken on July 29th, 1944, the day the Roncey Pocket was closed. An M7 Priest passes by the grave of SS Unterscharführer Josef Ritschfeld, killed on July 17th, 1944. This sergeant was from the 17th SS Panzergrenadier Division Götz von Berlichingen, one of the divisions surrounded at Roncey. (National Archives)

For the Germans, the second night of the breakout took on an atmosphere of "every man for himself." There were no concerted assaults, but kampfgruppen of varying sizes attacked towards the southeast, encountering Americans and managing to either break out or being forced to surrender.

During one of the most significant night-time battles, Panthers of the Das Reich Division managed to recapture Saint-Denis-le-Gast from the Americans. They held the village for several hours, allowing other troops to pass through, but in the ensuing confusion the kampfgruppe left its post and disappeared towards the south. Without them, the Americans soon retook the village.

The German losses were very heavy throughout the night. Martin Blumenson estimates the number of German dead at 1,500 (though this seems high) and the number of prisoners at 4,000. Hundreds of vehicles were abandoned.

Despite everything—and this prefigures the Falaise Pocket—many troops did in fact manage to escape, including the Panzer IV battalion of 2nd SS Panzer Division, the bulk of the 17th SS Panzergrenadier Division Götz von Berlichingen and part of the 6th Fallschirmjäger. The Das Reich Panthers also managed to get past the Americans, mostly on the first night, but their losses were heavier than the Panzer IV battalion's. The numerous troops that escaped were too exhausted to continue the fight and re-establish the front in the face of the Americans.

A Panther in the Pocket

Fritz Langanke, a Panther commander, wrote about the fighting in the Roncey Pocket. He recounted how he received an order to advance towards Percy (that is to say, southeast) on the evening of July 28th, and immediately ran into a terrible traffic jam, mostly made up of non-combat vehicles. He could not get through that evening and had to spend the day on the receiving end of aerial attacks, which remarkably caused no damage to the Panther, apart from a small fire in materials stored behind the turret. On the evening of the 29th, Langanke prepared to advance at the head of a small kampfgruppe:

> At the head was my tank, with Panzergrenadiers to the left and around 50 or 60 paratroopers to the right, to protect us from any enemy armed with bazookas. Next, two assault guns, wheeled vehicles from our kampfgruppe and a few others,

A Das Reich column destroyed near Mortain, including at least one Schwimmwagen and an Sd Kfz 251 Ausf D. (National Archives)

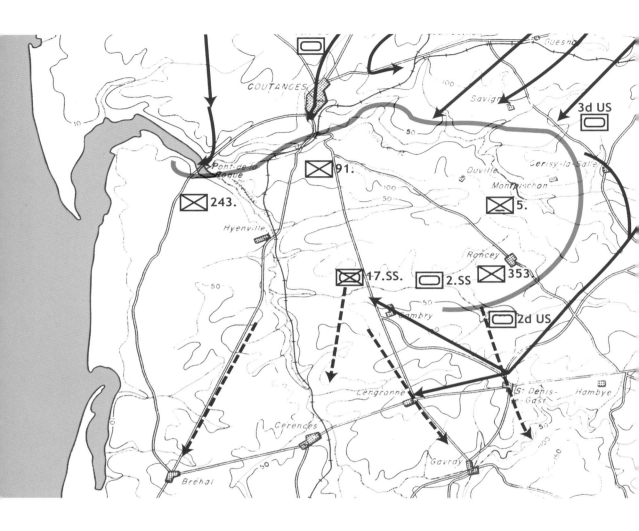

American armored divisions
German breakthrough attempts on night of 28th to 29th July
American advance
German front on evening of 28th July
Panzerdivision
Panzergrenadierdivision
Infanterie Division
Fallschirmjäger Division (parachutists)

Scale in kilometers

0   2 km   4 km   6 km

A pocket-map of Roncey (pun intended) and the positions of German divisions trying to break through the surrounding enemy lines.

self-propelled infantry guns and some mobile Flak batteries. Finally, bringing up the rear, a Panzer IV and a second Panther.

The departure took place at 2200hrs. At the outset, Langanke put a Sherman out of action, then, travelling at high speed down the Hambye–Roncey road, his Panther destroyed an American antitank gun. Langanke ordered his accompanying assault guns to attack two Shermans that he spotted, and after some hesitation they easily destroyed them.

The Germans had the element of surprise; soon, Langanke destroyed the last in a column of half-tracks, and filled with ammo, it flew into the air in a huge explosion that illuminated the night. He took advantage of this by firing on the other half-tracks, causing panic among the Americans. The Germans seized abandoned US vehicles to assist with transporting their own troops during the withdrawal.

Waffen-SS captured in Normandy. (US National Archives)

A Panzer Ausf G destroyed during the Ardennes Offensive.
The Das Reich Division managed to find 58 at the
beginning of the offensive.

An eight-wheeled German armored vehicle abandoned at a quay on the Danube in Budapest. The vehicle belonged to the Wehrmacht, not the Waffen-SS. The operation on Lake Balaton was halted before it got close to the Hungarian capital. (Rights reserved)

When the kampfgruppe finally reached Lengronne, it had doubled in size: from 300, the Germans now numbered 600, as various isolated and disparate units had joined Langanke along the way. The final test was crossing the damaged bridge at La Baleine. South of the river, the Germans were effectively safe as the area was defensively well organized with large pennants on the front lines indicating the locations of different units. The kampfgruppe was thence disbanded and its men permitted to rejoin their original units.

Langanke had been so successful in his mission that he was recommended for the Knight's Cross on August 7th, 1944. He received it on August 27th, and survived the war.

The Roncey Pocket, the first pocket in the battle for Normandy, had been caused by an error in the German command, as was the following, that of Falaise. The troops needed all their mettle to escape and resume the fight in the days that followed. In total, the Germans left around 5,000 prisoners in Roncey, which is not so many when one considers that six entire divisions were surrounded. Without doubt, the worst losses were those of matériel, especially transport vehicles, without which Germans actions were severely disrupted.

From Mortain to Falaise

The Das Reich Division suffered greatly in the last days of July, but nevertheless was employed in Operation *Lüttich*, the counterattack in the direction of Mortain, in order to sever Patton's Third Army from its supply lines.

The Cérences railway station after an American air raid. Though the bombs created huge craters, they were generally ineffective against tanks. The British said that during their investigations, at La Baleine, some tanks had been found intact on the edge of a crater. (National Archives)

The Das Reich formed three kampfgruppen: the principal effort would be made on the left wing, with support from the armored regiment. To the north, the Der Führer Regiment would circumvent Mortain.

The attack took place at night, principally against the US 30th Infantry Division. The groups to the north and center failed, but the group to the south managed to seize Mortain. The accomplishment was short-lived, however, as everywhere else it was failure after failure for the Germans. In daytime hours, rocket-firing Typhoons and other Allied aircraft ripped through the German formations. All that remained was to go on the defensive on the night of August 8th/9th, before retreating to avoid encirclement.

These German soldiers have not had Langanke's luck and that of his kampfgruppe. They were captured in the Roncey Pocket. According to their uniforms, there is a mix of paratroopers and members of the 17th SS-Panzergrenadier Division Götz von Berlichingen and 2nd SS-Panzer Division Das Reich. (National Archives)

In March 1945, a Russian soldier, armed with a racing bicycle and a PPsh submachine gun, carefully approaches a German 105mm gun in the ruins of Budapest.

A Königstiger II (Royal Tiger) destroyed during the fighting around Lake Balaton, from March 8th to March 16th, 1945. It was the final German offensive in the East. (Rights reserved)

By now the entire German front in Normandy was in retreat, as the British, Canadian, and American armies closed in from either side. The Das Reich Division managed to escape the Falaise Pocket before it closed, but then its armor was sent back in again to hold open a passage for following units to escape. This resulted in an epic battle against the 1st Polish Armored Division atop Montormel, or Hill 262. The 2nd SS Panzer was finally pulled out as rearguard in the retreat, its efforts having helped over 200,000 men to escape the Normandy disaster.

The division then retreated via Elbeuf, on the Seine, where it fought again with pursuing US units, and then on to the Meuse. It returned to the borders of the Reich on September 11th, 1944, with barely no remaining tanks. In mid-October, it was relieved from duty to be refitted. However, it would never recover the strength it had possessed in June 1944, and many units had to rely on bicycles for mobility.

A German 105mm model 18/40 howitzer, in perfect condition, abandoned with its shells by its crew during the last of the fighting in Prague.

The Ardennes

While preparing for the Ardennes Offensive, the Das Reich Division was replenished with the following strength in armor;

- 28 × StuG III;
- 28 × Panzer IV;
- 58 × Panther;
- 8 × Flakpanzer.

The beginnings of the offensive were particularly difficult for the division, which as part of the second assault wave crawled along the impractical roads, low on morale. Das Reich was blocked for more than three days before finally, on December 22nd, it attacked in the direction of the Meuse, in the Baraque de Fraiture. American resistance was strong and the progress minimal, despite German tanks causing heavy losses among their adversaries. On December 23rd, in retaliation for the loss of four Panzer IVs, they destroyed 17 Shermans and 34 half-tracks. The next day, Ernst Barkmann, of Normandy heroics, again launched a one-man massacre of the Shermans.

Manhay, the target for the division on the road to the Meuse, was finally taken, but the Americans, supported by overwhelming artillery, counterattacked and retook the village on December 26th. On the 27th, the Waffen-SS were forcibly driven back eastward. The division engaged in scattered fighting with elements of Patton's Third Army until on January 4th, 1945, all orders to attack were annulled and the division withdrew to the blockhouses of the Westwall on the border of the Reich.

Hungary

In February 1945, the 2nd SS Panzer Division departed the Western Front to participate in the offensive in Hungary to rescue Budapest from the Red Army and to safeguard Germany's last remaining oil fields. Its strength was further depleted from its December 1944 levels to:

- 28 × StuG III and IV;
- 26 × Panzer IV;
- 31 × Panther;
- 8 × Flakpanzer IV.

This represents around half of the division's armored strength in June 1944.

Operation *Spring Awakening* was launched in the region of Lake Balaton, with the aim of destroying the Russian armies located between the lake and the Danube: the Soviet 4th Guards Tank Army, the 26th and 57th armies and the 1st Bulgarian Army. This region had become essential to Germany, once it had lost its synthetic oil plants to air attack, as its sole source of natural production.

The offensive began on March 8th, in the morning. It was the last large-scale attack on the Eastern Front, yet it was hardly enough to worry the Russians, despite some initial successes and the futile sacrifice of Waffen-SS units. On March 16th, the Russians counterattacked and General Fyoder Tolbukhin, who commanded the 3rd Ukrainian Front, retook in one day everything that the Germans had taken a week to capture. The Das Reich Division, for the last time, was divided into several kampfgruppen, separated from each other by the Russian offensive.

Vienna fell on April 13th, 1945. The 2nd SS Panzer was completely broken up, with some elements fighting the Americans in Austria while others attempted to save civillians and support troops in Prague. The division, with only 5,000 men remaining following Operation *Spring Awakening*, received 2,800 sailors as reinforcements. On April 30th, with Russian troops at his doorstep in Berlin, Adolf Hitler committed suicide, and his successors arranged a formal surrender on May 8th. With the capitulation of the Third Reich, the Das Reich Division surrendered at Passau on the American front, though several kampfgruppen gave themselves up to the Russians at Dresden.

Afterword

From its beginnings as the Verfügungstruppe to its final incarnation as the 2nd SS Panzer Division, the unit we now know as "Das Reich" was veritably destroyed several times during World War II, yet was always rebuilt and returned to the fight—invariably where the battle was most crucial.

After the war a new campaign of recriminations began against German commanders, particularly those with a connection to the SS, once Nazi Germany's evil secret of the Holocaust became known. Thence began a lifelong campaign on the part of former Das Reich leaders such as Hausser and Steiner to establish that the Waffen-SS were front-line troops who sacrificed themselves in combat—not domestic henchmen of a murderous regime.

Given the ruthlessness of the war in Russia, and certain ramifications that carried over to the West, the lines were sometimes blurred. However, though often failed by high command, and sometimes split apart to act as stiffeners for other units, the combat performance of Das Reich has never been called into question. Through its ranks served a number of officers who achieved higher command, even as the rank-and-file established a reputation for battlefield prowess.

Further Reading

Balck, Hermann. *Order in Chaos: The Memoirs of General of Panzer Troops Hermann Balck*. Lexington, KY: The University Press of Kentucky, 2015.

Guderian, Heinz. *Panzer Leader*. New York: E.P. Dutton & Co., 1952.

Lucas, James. *Das Reich: The Military Role of the 2nd SS Division*. London: Arms and Armour Press, 1991.

Manstein, Erich von. *Lost Victories*. Novato, CA: Presidio Press, 1982.

Mattson, Gregory L. *SS-Das Reich: The History of the Second SS Division 1941–45*. London: Amber Books, 2002.

Mellenthin, F.W. von. *Panzer Battles: A Study of the Employment of Armor in the Second World War*. Norman, OK: University of Oklahoma Press, 1956.

Index

1st Bulgarian Army, 124
1st Polish Armored Division, 122

Anschluss, 15
Ardennes Offensive, 118, 123
Arnhem, 29, 33

Balaton, Lake, 4, 59, 62–63
Balck, Hermann, 79
Balkans campaign, 6, 23, 28
Barkmann, Unterscharführer Ernst, 106, 123
Baum, Otto, 108
Belgrade, 37
Berlin, 43, 51, 69, 79, 124
Bittrich, Wilhelm, 96
Blumenson, Martin, 57
Bochmann, Sturmbannführer Georg, 78
British Army *also* British Expeditionary
    Force, 95
        Queen's Own Royal West Kent Regiment,
        35
Budapest, 117, 121, 124
Bug river, 43

Calais, 34
Caucasus mountains, 51, 54–56, 71

Danube river, 37, 117, 124
Demelhüber, Untersturmführer Karl-Maria,
    20, 29
Diekmann, Adolf, 100
Dietrich, Oberst-Gruppenführer 'Sepp', 28
Dnieper river, 48, 55, 68, 71, 80, 95
DNVP *see* German National People's Party
Don river, 71
Donetz basin, 54–56
Dunkirk, 34–35, 95

Falaise Pocket, 7, 28, 112, 117, 122

German forces
Armies and army groups (Waffen-SS &
    Wehrmacht)
        6th SS Panzer Army (formerly 6th Panzer

Army), 28
Army Group A, 71
Army Group B, 69
Army Group Center, 6, 43, 54, 69, 95
Army Group North, 22
Army Group South, 7, 79–80, 90
Eighteenth Army, 29
Fourth Panzer Army, 36, 42, 44, 89, 94
Sixth Army, 71, 83
Corps and panzer groups (Waffen-SS &
    Wehrmacht)
        1st Panzer Group, 48, 56
        2nd Panzer Group *also* Panzer Group
        Guderian, 40, 42, 48, 68–69
        Afrikakorps, 37
        II SS Panzer Corps, 83, 86, 96
        SS Panzer Corps, 7, 28, 71, 76–79, 83–84,
        86, 89
        VIII Army Corps, 22
        XLI Panzer Corps, 68
        XXIV Army Corps, 43
Divisions (Waffen-SS)
        1st SS Panzer Division Leibstandarte SS
        Adolf Hitler, 71, 76–77, 83, 90
        2nd SS Panzer Division Das Reich
        (previously SS Verfügungs Division, later
        SS Panzergrenadier Division Das Reich),
        7, 10, 17, 43, 47, 50, 65, 71–72, 74, 76–78,
        80, 83–90, 92, 95–97, 100, 102, 104, 107–
        110, 112, 117, 122–126
            Artillery Regiment, 44, 56, 103–104
            Der Führer Regiment, 45, 57, 60, 63–65,
            74, 77, 83, 94–95, 118
            Deutschland Regiment, 37, 43, 45, 56–
            57, 60, 63, 82–83, 86, 95
            Langemarck Regiment, 65
        3rd SS Panzer Division Totenkopf
        (previously SS Panzergrenadier Division
        Totenkopf), 71, 78, 80, 82–83, 90
            6th SS Panzergrenadier Regiment
            Theodor Eicke, 78
            Standarte 41 Allgemeine SS Bayreuth, 7
        5th SS Panzer Division Wiking (previously
        SS Panzergrenadier Division Wiking)

Germania Regiment,
9th SS Panzer Division Hohenstaufen, 100
12th SS Panzer Division Hitlerjugend, 95
17th SS Panzergrenadier Division Götz von Berlichingen, 107, 112, 119
SS Verfüfungs (V) Division *see also* 2nd SS Panzer Division Das Reich, 6, 13, 17, 22–25, 28–29, 33–34, 36, 39, 125
SS Leibstandarte Adolf Hitler, 13, 15, 17–18, 21, 42
I. SS Standarte Deutschland/VT, 13, 15, 17–18, 20–22, 29, 34, 42
II. SS Standarte Germania/VT, 15, 17, 35
III. SS Standarte Der Führer/VT, 15, 17, 29, 32, 35
Divisions (Wehrmacht)
10th Panzer Division, 48, 56, 60
207th Infantry Division, 29
243rd Infantry Division, 107
268th Infantry Division, 48
320th Infantry Division, 76
353rd Infantry Division, 100, 107
3rd Panzer Division, 68–69, 90
5th Fallschirmjäger Division, 107
6th Fallschirmjäger Regiment, 109, 112
6th Panzer Division, 68, 74
91st Air Landing Division, 107
Panzer Division Kempf, 22
Kampfgruppen (Waffen-SS & Wehrmacht)
Kampfgruppe Förster, 48
Kampfgruppe Grave, 29
Kampfgruppe Lamerding, 102
Kampfgruppe Reich, 64
Kampfgruppe Weldinger, 100
German National People's Party (DNVP), 12
Guderian, General Heinz, 11, 43, 52, 55–56, 68–69
Gzhatsk, 56–57, 63

Harmel, Heinz, 74
Hausser, Generaloberst Paul, 28, 37, 42, 51, 77–78, 80, 96, 106, 108, 125
Heer (German Regular Army), 15, 17
Hengl, Ritter von, 17
Hess, Rudolf, 18
Himmler, Reichsführer SS Heinrich, 11, 13, 17–18, 20, 36, 70, 88, 96
Hindenburg, President Paul von, 12
Hitler Youth, 70

Hitler, Adolf, 7, 10–13, 17–18, 20–22, 28, 37, 42, 48, 51, 54, 56, 60, 64–65, 69, 71, 74, 76–80, 83, 89, 94, 96, 110, 124
Hoth, General Hermann, 87, 89

Ijssel river, 29
Istra river, 60, 63

Keppler, Gruppenführer, 77
Kharkov, *also* Battle of, 28, 46, 52, 56, 70–71, 76–80, 82, 88, 90, 92, 94–97
Kiev, *also* pocket, 6, 48, 52, 54–56, 69, 71
Kleinheisterkamp, Matthias, 29, 96
Kleist, General von, 52, 56
Klingenberg, Hauptsturmführer Fritz, 37
Kluge, Field Marshal von, 106
Kommunistische Partei Deutschlands (KPD), 10
Krüger, Obergruppenführer Walter, 96–97
Kumm, Obersturmbannführer Otto, 63–64
Kursk, *also* Battle of, 7, 28, 46, 52, 73, 76–77, 79–80, 82–83, 85–89, 91, 94–95, 97

Laackmann, Sturmbannführer Anton, 78
Laborde, Admiral, 65–66
Lammerding, Heinz, 96
Langanke, Fritz, 113, 115, 117, 119
Luftwaffe, 37, 86, 103

Manstein, General Erich von, 7, 71, 79–80, 94, 96
Maquis, 100
Meuse river, 122–123
Minsk, 44–45, 52
Mlava, 22
Model, General Walter, 64, 68–69, 87, 89, 96
Modlin Fortress, 22
Mortain, 113, 117–118
Moscow, *also* Battle of, 6, 45, 47–48, 52, 54, 56–57, 60, 63, 69
Mussolini, 20

National Socialist German Worker's Party (NSDAP), 10, 12–13
Nieppe Forest, 35
Nijmegen, 29, 33
Normandy landings, 7, 28, 69, 95–96, 100, 109, 117, 123
Nuremberg, 9, 16–17

Operations
    Barbarossa, 6, 28, 38, 41, 43, 49, 52, 54, 69,
      79, 84, 95
    Citadel, 76, 82–83, 89
    Cobra, 96, 106
    Epsom, 100
    Lila, 66
    Lüttich, 117
    Market Garden, 33, 96
    Spring Awakening, 124
    Typhoon, 56, 68
    Uranus, 83
    Fall Weiss, 22
Oradour-sur-Glane, 100–101

Papen, Franz von, 12
Patton, General, 117, 123
Politische Bereitschaften, 10, 13
Prague, 123–124
Pripet marshes, 43

Red Army
    1st Army, 82
    1st Tank Corps, 86
    24th Army, 48
    102nd Armoured Division, 48
    26th Army, 124
    3rd Ukrainian Front, 124
    32nd Siberian Infantry Division, 57
    4th Guards Tank Army, 124
    5th Guards Tank Army, 87
    57th Army, 124
    7th Guards Cavalry Corps, 78
    Stavka Strategic Reserves, 48, 71, 78,
      82–83, 86
Reichsparteitag, 14
Reichstag, 10–11
Ritschfeld, Unterscharführer Josef, 112
Rommel, Field Marshal Erwin, 37, 100, 103
Roncey Pocket, 101, 103–109, 112–117, 119
Röske, Hauptscharführer, 35
Rostov, 71
Rühl, Heid, 44–45
Rzhev, 52, 63–64

Saint-Lô, 106

Schümann, Paul, 32
Schützstaffel (SS), 10
    Allgemeine SS, 7, 10, 13, 17
Seine river, 122
Seventh Army (French), 29
Sienne river, 107–108
Smolensk, 44–45, 52, 57
Speer, Albert, 11
Stadler, Sturmbannführer, 77
Stalingrad, *also* Battle of, 7, 51, 71, 79, 83, 95,
    96
Steiner, Obergruppenführer Felix, 36, 42, 51,
    96, 125
Sturmabteilung (SA 'Brownshirts'), 9, 11–12
Sudetenland, 20

Tannenberg, Battle of, 22
Tolbukhin, General Fyoder, 124
Tomić, Jevrem, 37
Toulon see also Operation *Lila*, 7, 31, 65–66
Treaty of Versailles, 12, 17
Tulle, 100
Tychsen, Obersturmführer Christian, 96, 108

Ulrich, Sturmbannführer Karl, 78
US Army
    Third (US) Army, 117, 123
    VII Corps, 107
      2nd Armored Division, 96, 99, 107
      3rd Armored Division, 106, 109
      4th Infantry Division, 109
      30th Infantry Division, 118

Vienna, 15, 124
Vistula river, 43
Volga river, 64

Waal river, 29
Walcheren, 29, 33–34
Weygand line, 36
Witt, Fritz, 77

Yelnia, 45, 48, 57

Zhukov, Marshal Georgy, 48, 60, 64